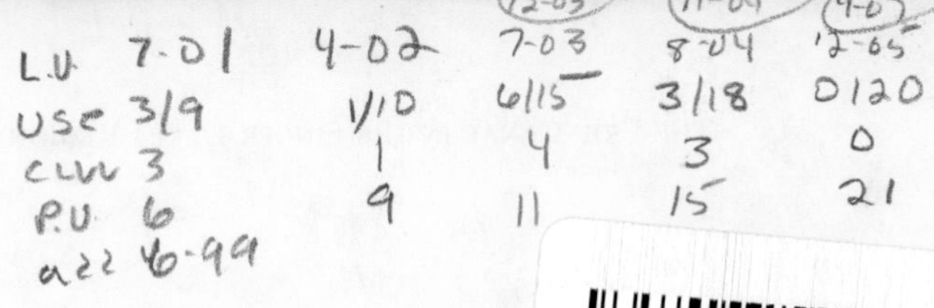

The Erie Canal in the Finger Lakes Region

The Heart of New York State

By Emerson Klees

Photography by C. S. Kenyon

Friends of the Finger Lakes Publishing, Rochester, New York

For information, write:

Friends of the Finger Lakes Publishing
P.O. Box 18131
Rochester, New York 14618

Library of Congress Catalog Card Number 96-61439

ISBN 0-9635990-2-X
Printed in the United States of America
9 8 7 6 5 4 3 2 1

Cover design and book design by Seneca Mist Graphics, Ithaca, NY
Designer, Dru Wheelin/Final Production by Terry Porcelli-VanDyke

Preface

THE ERIE CANAL IN THE FINGER LAKES REGION: The Heart of New York State provides general information about the Erie Canal and specific information about the canal in Monroe, Wayne, Cayuga, and Onondaga counties. The Heart of New York State is bounded by the I-390 Expressway in the West, the New York State Thruway in the North, the I-81 Expressway and Route 13 in the East, and Route 17, the Southern Tier Expressway, in the South. The scenic Finger Lakes Region is comprised of fourteen counties, 264 municipalities, and 6,125 square miles.

The Prologue discusses the proposals to build waterways during the 100 years preceding the canal's completion in 1825. The Introduction provides a brief history of the building of the canal. Also included in the book are short biographies of seven people who were instrumental in planning and building the canal, eight stories depicting life on the canal, and a description and brief history of the villages along the canal in the region.

The book also contains information about places to see and things to do along a thirty-mile-wide strip across the northern section of the Finger Lakes Region—fifteen miles north of the canal to Lake Ontario and fifteen miles south of the canal to Routes 5 and 20. (In the *New York State Canal Recreationway Plan*, fifteen miles is described as the distance a hiker might walk in a half-day or a biker or boater might travel in a day, one way.) The thirty-mile-wide strip is shaded in the map on the reverse side of the Preface. The Epilogue summarizes plans for the future of the canal as outlined in the *New York State Canal Recreationway Plan* of 1995, including modifications in 1996.

This book includes some material reprinted from *PERSONS, PLACES, AND THINGS IN THE FINGER LAKES REGION* and *PERSONS, PLACES, AND THINGS AROUND THE FINGER LAKES REGION*. Two books that provide useful information from the boaters' viewpoint are the *ERIE CANAL GUIDE: Western Section—Tonawanda to Syracuse* by Jeremy G. Frankel and Capt. Peter Wiles, Jr., and *THE NEW ERIE CANAL: A Recreational Guide* by John R. Fitzgerald.

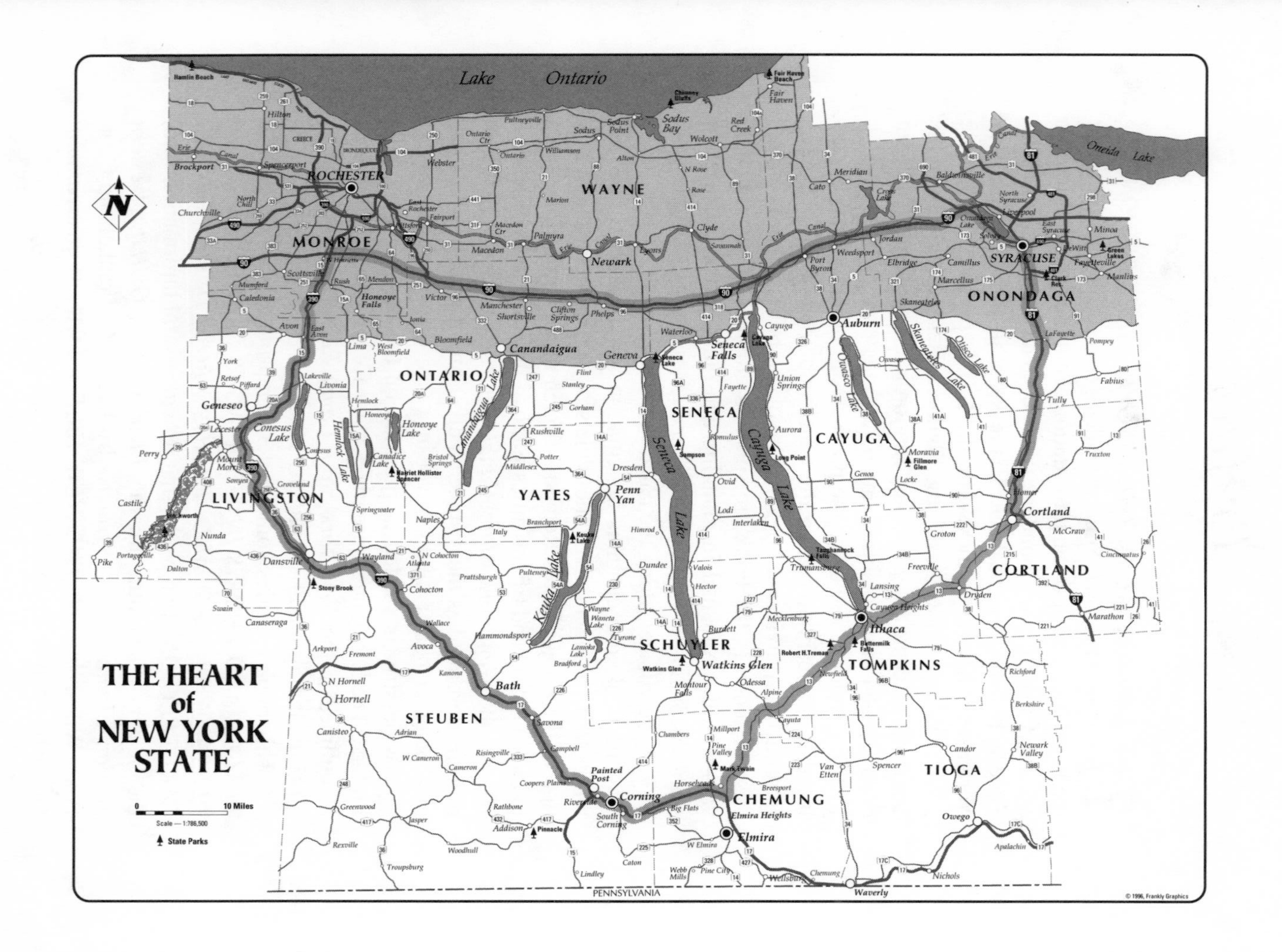
THE HEART of NEW YORK STATE
Lake Ontario
Oneida Lake
ROCHESTER
SYRACUSE
MONROE
WAYNE
ONONDAGA
CAYUGA
SENECA
ONTARIO
YATES
LIVINGSTON
SCHUYLER
TOMPKINS
CORTLAND
TIOGA
CHEMUNG
STEUBEN
Skaneateles Lake
Owasco Lake
Otisco Lake
Cayuga Lake
Seneca Lake
Keuka Lake
Canandaigua Lake
Honeoye Lake
Canadice Lake
Hemlock Lake
Conesus Lake
Auburn
Ithaca
Cortland
Elmira
Corning
Bath
Geneva
Canandaigua
Newark
Seneca Falls
Watkins Glen
Penn Yan
Geneseo
Dansville
Hornell
Owego
Waverly
Painted Post
PENNSYLVANIA
State Parks
10 Miles
© 1996, Frankly Graphics

List of Photographs

Front cover—Schoen Place, Pittsford

Back Cover—Camillus Erie Canal Park

Inside the Book		Page No.
1.	Aqueduct Park, Palmyra	vi
2.	Centreport Aqueduct, near Weedsport	xiv
3.	Nine Mile Creek Aqueduct, Camillus	6
4.	Lock 32, Pittsford	14
5.	Canalboat, Erie Canal Museum, Syracuse	31
6.	Packett's Landing, Fairport	32
7.	Stump Puller illustration by Dru Wheelin	54
8.	Erie Canal at Adams Basin	58
9.	Main Street, Brockport	82
10.	Lock 30, Macedon	89
11.	Granger Homestead, Canandaigua	101
12.	Hill Cumorah / Moroni Monument, south of Palmyra	107
13.	Sodus Bay Lighthouse Museum, Sodus Point	121
14.	Rose Hill Mansion, Geneva	130
15.	Geneva-on-the-Lake	139
16.	Women's Rights National Historical Park Visitor Center, Seneca Falls	148
17.	Memorial Day Museum, Waterloo	156
18.	Willard Memorial Chapel, Auburn	174
19.	Tour Boats on Skaneateles Lake	194
20.	Sherwood Inn, Skaneateles	198
21.	Lock 26, Clyde	209
22.	Main Street, Fairport	210
23.	Waterway Crane, Lock 25, Mays Point	214

Aqueduct Park, Palmyra

Table of Contents

Preface iii

List of Photographs v

Table of Contents vii

Prologue—Proposals for a Canal 1

Introduction—Building the Canal 7

Chapter 1—People of the Erie Canal 15
- DeWitt Clinton 16
- James Geddes 18
- Jesse Hawley 19
- Gouverneur Morris 23
- Nathan Roberts 25
- Canvass White 27
- Benjamin Wright 29

Chapter 2—Erie Canal Stories 33
- Life on the Canal 34
- A Little White Lie 37
- The Montezuma Mosquitoes 44
- Pilkington's Four-Skate Escapade 46
- Repairing a Breach 49
- The Stump Puller 53
- Tyrone Power's Trip on the Canal 55
- Workers from Ireland 56

Chapter 3—Villages along the Canal, West to East 59

Brockport 60
Adams Basin 64
Spencerport 65
Rochester (south of) 67
Pittsford 68
Bushnells Basin 69
Fairport 70
Macedon 71
Palmyra 72
Newark 74
Lyons 76
Clyde 77
Baldwinsville 79
Brewerton 80

PLACES TO SEE AND THINGS TO DO ALONG THE CANAL 83

Chapter 4—From Canandaigua to Lake Ontario 91

North of the Canal 95
Places to See 95
1) Robert E. Ginna Nuclear Power Plant 95
Things to Do 96
2) Williamson International Speedway 96
South of the Canal 96
Places to See 96
West of Canandaigua 96
3) Valentown Museum of Local History 96
4) Electronics Communications Museum 98
5) Ganondagan State Historic Site 99
Canandaigua 99
6) Granger Homestead and Carriage Museum 99

7) Ontario County Historical Society Museum 102
8) Sonnenberg Gardens and Mansion 102
9) Canandaigua Lake State Marine Park 104
10) Kershaw Park 104
11) Finger Lakes Community College 104

Palmyra 105
12) Alling Coverlet Museum 105
13) Palmyra Historical Museum 106
14) William Phelps General Store Museum 106
15) Hill Cumorah and the Moroni Monument 106
16) Historic Grandin Building 108
17) Joseph Smith Home 108
18) Martin Harris Farm 108
19) The Sacred Grove 109

Things to Do 109

Canandaigua 109
20) Finger Lakes Performing Arts Center 109
21) New York Pageant of Steam 110
22) Canandaigua Speedway 110
23) Boat Rides on the *Canandaigua Lady* 110
24) Captain Gray's Boat Tours 111
25) Thendara Inn—Historic Restaurant and Inn 111

Between Canandaigua and the Canal 112
26) Finger Lakes Race Track 112
27) The Hill Cumorah Pageant 112
28) The Wild Water Derby 114
29) Holloway House—Historic Restaurant 115

CHAPTER 5—FROM GENEVA TO LAKE ONTARIO **117**

North of the Canal 119

Places to See 119
30) Blue Cut Nature Center 119
31) Sodus Bay Lighthouse Museum 120

32) Wayne County Historical Society Museum 122
33) Chimney Bluffs State Park 122
34) Galen Marsh State Wildlife Management Area 123
Things to Do 124
35) Alasa Farms 124
36) Sodus Shaker Festival 124
37) *Liberty* Erie Canal Cruises 125
South of the Canal 126
Places to See 126
Between Geneva and the Canal 126
38) Amberg Wine Cellars 126
39) Hoffman Clock Museum 126
Geneva 127
40) Seneca Lake State Park 127
41) Hobart / William Smith Colleges 128
42) Prouty-Chew Museum 128
43) Rose Hill Mansion 129
44) Mike Weaver Drain Tile Museum 132
Things to Do 133
Between Geneva and the Canal 133
45) Sauerkraut Festival 133
Geneva 134
46) Smith Opera House 134
47) Boat Rides on the *Seneca Dreamer* 135
48) Belhurst Castle—Historic Restaurant and Inn 135
49) Geneva-on-the-Lake—Resort 137

CHAPTER 6—FROM SENECA FALLS / WATERLOO TO LAKE ONTARIO **141**
North of the Canal 145
Places to See 145
50) Thorpe Vineyard and Farm Winery 145

51) Lake Shore Marshes Wildlife Management Area 145
South of the Canal 146
Places to See 146
Seneca Falls 146
52) Elizabeth Cady Stanton House 146
53) National Women's Hall of Fame 147
54) Women's Rights National Historic Park Visitor Center 147
55) Wesleyan Chapel 149
56) Urban Cultural Park—Village of Seneca Falls 149
57) Seneca Falls Historical Society Museum 150
58) New York Chiropractic College 151
59) Cayuga Lake State Park 151
60) Montezuma National Wildlife Refuge 151
Waterloo 154
61) The Scythe Tree 154
62) Peter Whitmer Home 155
63) Memorial Day Museum 155
Things to Do 157
Seneca Falls 157
64) Convention Days 157
65) Empire State Farm Days 157

CHAPTER 7—FROM AUBURN TO LAKE ONTARIO **159**
North of the Canal 161
Places to See 161
66) Fair Haven Beach State Park 161
67) Howland Island State Wildlife Management Area 162
Things to Do 164
68) Sterling Renaissance Festival 164

South of the Canal 165
Places to See 165
Between Auburn and the Canal 165
69) DIRT Motorsport Hall of Fame and Classic Car Collection 165
70) Cayuga County Fair Speedway 165
Auburn 166
71) Fort Hill Cemetery 166
72) The Seward House 167
73) Harriet Tubman House 170
74) Cayuga County Agricultural Museum 171
75) Owasco Teyetasta (Iroquois Museum) 171
76) Cayuga Museum of History and Art 171
77) Schweinfurth Memorial Art Center 172
78) Willard Memorial Chapel 173
79) Cayuga Community College 176
80) Casey Park 176
81) Cayuga Community College Trail 177
82) Emerson Park 177
Things to Do 177
83) Auburn Concert Series 177
84) Merry-Go-Round Playhouse 177
85) Antique / Classic Boat Show 178
86) Finger Lakes Antique Car Show 178
87) Springside Inn—Historic Restaurant and Inn 178

CHAPTER 8—FROM SKANEATELES TO OSWEGO COUNTY 181
North of the Canal 183
Places to See 183
88) Beaver Lake Nature Center 183
89) Three Rivers State Wildlife Management Area 184

South of the Canal 185
Places to See 185
East of Skaneateles 185
90) Camillus Erie Canal Park 185
91) Erie Canal Museum, Syracuse 185
Between Skaneateles and the Canal 186
92) Carpenter's Brook Fish Hatchery 186
93) Wooden Toy Factory 186
Skaneateles 187
94) Austin Park 187
95) Baltimore Woods 187
96) Skaneateles Nature Trail 188
97) Thayer Park 188
98) John D. Barrow Art Gallery 188
99) Skaneateles Historical Association Museum—The Creamery 189
Things to Do 190
Between Skaneateles and the Canal 190
100) Rolling Wheels Track 190
Skaneateles 190
101) Skaneateles Art Exhibition 190
102) The Skaneateles Festival 190
103) Skaneateles Polo Club 191
104) Mid-Lakes Navigation Ltd. Cruises 192
105) The Krebs—Historic Restaurant 195
106) The Sherwood Inn—Historic Restaurant and Inn 197

Epilogue—The Future of the Erie Canal **199**

Bibliography **211**

Index **215**

Centreport Aqueduct, near Weedsport

• *prologue* •

"Why sir, here is a canal of a few miles projected by General Washington, which if completed, would render this (Washington, D.C.) a fine commercial city, which has languished for many years, because the small sum of two hundred thousand dollars necessary to complete it cannot be obtained from the General Government, the State Government, or from individuals, and you talk of making a canal 350 miles through the wilderness! It is little short of madness to think of it at this day."

President Thomas Jefferson's reply in January 1809 to Joshua Forman of New York who had requested federal funds to build the Erie Canal. President Jefferson thought that it was "a very fine project that might be executed a century hence."

Proposals for a Canal

In 1714, Cadwallader Colden, Surveyor-General of the Province of New York, included in his report to Governor Burnet comments on access to Lake Ontario via the Onondaga River: "Besides the passage by the lakes, there is a river which comes from the country of the Senecas and falls into the Onondaga River, by which we have an easy carriage into the country without going near Ontario Lake. The head of this river goes near Lake Erie and probably may give a very near passage into that lake...." This was the first recorded speculation of a navigable connection between the Mohawk River and Lake Erie across the interior of the state thus avoiding Lake Ontario.

The Mohawk Valley gap in the Appalachian chain was the obvious route for a waterway across the state. Differences of opinion occurred about the area west of the head of the Mohawk River. Many visionaries proposed a route to Lake Ontario using the Oswego River. This route was strongly opposed because the use of Lake Ontario would open trade routes for Canada and the French.

In 1768, Sir Henry Moore, Governor of the Province of New York, in a message to the Colonial Legislature, proposed improving the navigation of the Mohawk River by the removing obstructions and the construction of sluices between Schenectady and Fort Stanwix (now Rome). In 1785, Christopher Colles, an Irish-born engineer, wrote *Proposals for the Settlement of the State of New York,* in which he suggested that a canal from the Hudson River to the Great Lakes was feasible. The State Assembly provided Colles with $125 to prepare a plan for removing obstructions from the Mohawk River.

In 1788, after attending the negotiations of the second Fort Stanwix Treaty, Elkanah Watson proposed to Senator Philip Schuyler and Governor George Clinton that Wood Creek, a tributary of Oneida Lake, and the Mohawk River could be connected by a short ditch. In March 1791, the State Legislature ordered "a survey of the land between the Mohawk River and Wood Creek at Fort Stanwix and an estimate to be made of the expense necessary to float loaded boats of a ton and a half burden, and to report to the Legislature."

In September 1791, Jonas Platt, the clerk of Herkimer County, met Abraham Hardenburgh and Benjamin Wright, who surveyed land suitable for a ditch between the Mohawk River and Wood Creek. A few days later, Stephen Bayard, General Van Cortlandt, Jeremiah Van Renssalaer, and Elkanah Watson passed through Whitestown to investigate improvements in the water route from Schenectady to Seneca Falls.

Philip Schuyler and his partners formed the Western Inland Lock Navigation Company to take the first steps toward building a waterway to the West. The two largest impediments to navigation on the Mohawk River were the rocky rapids at Little Falls and the 200-foot drop at Cohoes Falls near the mouth of the river. At Little Falls, the Western Inland Lock Navigation Company built a mile-long canal with five locks, each with a lift of nine feet, to maneuver boats around the rapids. A bypass canal, called "Schuyler's Ditch," was built on the lower Mohawk at Cohoes Falls.

When Thomas Eddy, a member of the Western Inland Lock Navigation Company, was asked to find an engineer who could build flood dams and sluices, he wrote to Jonas Platt. Platt responded that James Geddes of Syracuse was an able engineer, but, since he wasn't available, Benjamin Wright of Rome would be an excellent choice. Wright made proposals and conducted a survey, but the Navigation Company couldn't afford to implement his proposals, even though they approved of them.

In 1803, Gouverneur Morris, who had been the U.S. Minister to France and a U.S. Senator, became interested in a canal across the state and traveled to Lake Erie to further develop his ideas. Morris proposed to Simeon DeWitt, the Surveyor-General of New York State, the idea of tapping the water of Lake Erie and building "an artificial river directly across the country to the Hudson River." At a time when no survey had been made of the western section of the proposed canal route to Buffalo, Morris proposed the use of an inclined plane instead of locks. This idea proved to be impractical.

Using the pen-name "Hercules," Jesse Hawley published an essay in the Pittsburgh *Commonwealth* in 1807, proposing a canal between Lake Erie and the Mohawk and Hudson rivers. He also published fourteen essays in the Canandaigua *Genesee Messenger* entitled "Observation on Canals." Hawley wrote, "I first conceived of the overland route of the canal, from Buffalo to Utica ... in 1805." He documented the idea in a letter to a friend.

In 1808, State Legislator Joshua Forman suggested that the Lake Erie Canal route should be surveyed. Surveyor-General DeWitt commissioned James Geddes to undertake the project. When Geddes had completed the survey, he agreed with Forman that the canal's western terminus should be Lake Erie, not Lake Ontario. Forman went to Washington in an unsuccessful bid to obtain federal funds from President Jefferson for a canal.

DeWitt Clinton, the mayor of New York City, read Geddes' report of his surveys and was impressed. He became the canal's strongest supporter and seconded the resolution to appoint a commission to study the feasibility of building a canal across the state. He served on the commission, which was formed in 1810, with Simeon DeWitt, Thomas Eddy, William North, Peter B. Porter, and Stephen Van Rensselaer. Gouverneur Morris was the chairman of the commission.

The commissioners traveled across the state in 1811 to investigate the alternative canal routes. They estimated that the canal would cost $5 million, and they agreed that its western terminus should be Lake Erie. In 1812, Morris and Clinton made a second attempt to obtain federal funds for New York State's canal project. This time, President Madison rejected New York's request.

In 1814, the English engineer William Weston was engaged by the Canal Commission to study further the route of the proposed canal. In February 1817, Governor Daniel Tompkins resigned his office to assume the duties of the office of Vice President of the United States, to which he had been elected the previous November, giving DeWitt Clinton the opportunity to serve as governor. As governor of New York State, Clinton was in a position to push his favorite project, building the Erie Canal.

In early 1817, the State Legislature passed the bill approving the construction of the Erie Canal, and, in June of that year, the Canal Commission received bids for work on the waterway and handed out contracts. On July 4, 1817, Governor Clinton dug the first spadeful of earth for the canal at Rome, and New York was on its way to becoming the Empire State. According to Samuel Eliot Morrison in *The Oxford History of the American People,* "The Erie Canal ... made New York the Empire State."

◆ ◆ ◆

Nine Mile Creek Aqueduct, Camillus

· introduction ·

Governor DeWitt Clinton's Dream

"As a bond of union between the Atlantic and Western states, it may prevent the dismemberment of the American Empire. As an organ of communication between the Hudson, the Mississippi, the St. Lawrence, the Great Lakes of the North and the West and their tributary rivers, it will create the greatest inland trade ever witnessed. The most fertile and extensive regions of America will avail themselves of its facilities for a market. All their surplus productions, whether of the soil, the forest, the mines, or the water, their fabrics of art and their supplies of foreign commodities, will concentrate in the city of New York, for transportation abroad or consumption at home. Agriculture, manufacture, commerce, trade, navigation, and the arts will receive a correspondent encouragement.

The city will, in the course of time, become the granary of the world, the emporium of commerce, the seat of manufactures, the focus of great moneyed operations, and the concentrating point of vast, disposable, and accumulating capitals, which will stimulate, enliven, extend, and reward the exertions of human labor and ingenuity, in all their processes and exhibitions. And before the revolution of a century, the whole island of Manhattan, covered with inhabitants and replenished with a dense population, will constitute one vast city."

Building the Canal

On July 4, 1817, construction of the eighty-three-lock Erie Canal along a 364-mile route from Albany to Buffalo began at Rome. Dignitaries made speeches and turned over a spadeful of earth as cannons boomed and the crowd cheered. The ninety-four-mile section of the canal from Rome west to the Seneca River was chosen to be constructed first because it had a long, flat stretch of favorable terrain that required only six locks. Also, Rome was the village nearest the upper limit of navigation on the Mohawk River; the land was less rocky and easier to dig than other sections; and the landowners were more receptive.

Local contractors were responsible for constructing specific lengths of the canal. Contractors had no problem finding men who would work for eighty cents a day and "found" (room and board). Contractors were responsible not only for feeding the men and providing bunk houses that accommodated from twenty-four to forty men, but also for providing them with horses, tools, and their daily ration of whiskey.

In 1818, the first Irish workers began to work on the canal; eventually, they made up about a quarter of the work force. The workers grew tired of eating wild game and demanded beef, mutton, and pork. Stump pullers, scoops for lifting loose earth, special wheel barrows, and other tools were invented to help with the construction of the canal.

The prism or ditch of the original canal was forty feet wide at the top, twenty-eight feet wide at the bottom, and was only four feet deep. Along one side of the canal, a towpath ten feet wide was built for the horses and mules to pull the boats, and a berm was constructed along the other side. Over 300 "occupational" bridges were built over the canal. Unfortunately, the bridges, which allowed the owners of the property joined by the bridges to continue with their occupation (farming), were only seven and a half feet above the water level.

In 1818, Canvass White went to England to study canal-building techniques. He traveled 2,000 miles to study Europe's canals. The Languedoc Canal across southern France, which connected the Atlantic Ocean with the Mediterranean Sea, was the largest. When it opened in 1691, it had 119 locks and traversed 144 miles with aqueducts and tunnels as well as channels. White observed the Europeans' use of hydraulic cement that hardened when exposed to water.

Because it was expensive to import the cement to the United States, White came home and experimented with many formulae of burned limestone and sand. He developed a hydraulic cement that was made with limestone from Chittenango, which would set underwater like the expensive European cement. His breakthrough, which he patented, saved considerable time and money in constructing the canal.

In October 1819, another crowd gathered at Rome to celebrate the opening of the first section of the canal, the fifteen-mile section between Rome and Utica. Another eight miles of canal in the middle section had been completed but hadn't been inspected, another forty-eight miles had been dug, and all ninety-four miles of the section had been cleared. The canalboat *Chief Engineer of Rome,* named for Benjamin Wright who with James Geddes had made the early canal surveys, traveled from Rome to Utica that day and back the next.

On July 4, 1820, seventy-three new canalboats left Syracuse for Rome to celebrate the completion of the middle section of the canal.

The western end of the middle section was the most difficult to dig because of the Montezuma Marshes at the northern end of Cayuga Lake. At one point, malaria-carrying mosquitoes caused 1,000 workers to be unfit for work. The banks of a section of canal dug in the marshes would collapse into the canal overnight; extensive pilings had to be built to keep the banks in place.

The canal builders constructed eighteen aqueducts to carry the canal over rivers and streams. The most notable were the aqueduct at Schenectady that carried the canal 1,188 feet over twenty-six stone piers, a 744-foot-long aqueduct at Little Falls with three stone arches thirty feet high, and the 802-foot-long aqueduct over the Genesee River at Rochester that was constructed with nine Roman arches. Carrying the canal over the Irondequoit Valley near Rochester presented another challenge to the canal builders.

Engineers had to contend with a difference in elevation of 568 feet between Lake Erie and the Hudson River. Two of the most difficult projects during the construction were digging through rock in the eastern section of the canal near Albany and accommodating a sixty-foot drop in elevation at Lockport. Nathan Roberts solved the problem at Lockport with a double set of five-step locks, one set of locks each for eastbound and westbound traffic.

Clinton's original promise of completing the canal in 1823 at a cost of $5 million was not met. However, the canal from Rochester to Albany was opened in 1823; the cost of shipping a barrel of flour between those two cities dropped from $3.00 to 75¢. During the summer of 1824, 1,822 boats were operating on a forty-five-mile section of the canal near Rochester, from which $21,000 in tolls had been collected in six months. By the end of summer that year, a total of $300,000 in tolls had been collected from the sections of the canal that were in operation.

The full length of the Erie Canal was opened in 1825 with the ceremonial Buffalo to Albany cruise of Governor DeWitt Clinton on the *Seneca Chief,* accompanied by four other canalboats. Two barrels of water were transported by the Governor to pour into New York harbor, symbolizing the joining of Lake Erie and the Atlantic Ocean. One barrel held Lake Erie water, and the other contained water from the Amazon, Columbia, Gambia, Ganges, Indus, LaPlata, Mississippi, Nile, Orinoco, Rhine, Seine, and Thames rivers.

On board the steamship *Washington,* the New York City Common Council hailed the Governor's ship as the *Seneca Chief* approached New York. They asked, "Whence come you, and where are you bound?" The *Seneca Chief* replied, "From Lake Erie, bound for Sandy Hook!" At Rochester, the *Seneca Chief* had given a more lengthy reply:

> *"Who comes there?" the captain was asked as his boat approached the aqueduct over the Genesee River.*
>
> *"Your brothers from the West on the waters of the Great Lakes," replied the captain.*
>
> *"By what means have they been diverted from their natural course?"*
>
> *"Through the channel of the great Erie Canal."*
>
> *"By whose authority and by whom was a work of such magnitude accomplished?"*
>
> *"By the authority and by the enterprise of the people of the State of New York!"*

Most New Yorkers had not considered the $7,000,000 spent to build the canal ($2,000,000 over the original estimate) a good expenditure. They were proved wrong. The canal was economically successful beyond even Governor Clinton's dreams.

The increase in the use of the canal outstripped its capacity; traffic jams became commonplace. Between 1835 and 1862, many changes were made in the canal to facilitate the increased traffic: the width at the top of the canal was increased from 40 feet to 70 feet, the width at the bottom was expanded from 28 to 56 feet, and the depth was increased from 4 feet to 7 feet. In addition, the waterway was straightened, the number of locks was reduced from 83 to 72, and at most lock locations a double lock was built to allow two-way traffic.

By the beginning of the twentieth century, railroads were providing stiff competition for the Erie Canal. Canal managers wanted to take advantage of advanced engineering skills and steam tugboats. Construction began in 1905 to increase lock sizes to 45 feet wide by 328 feet long, reduce the number of locks from 72 to 35, and increase the depth of the canal from 7 feet to 12 feet.

Many of the rivers along the route of the canal that were not utilized during earlier construction were incorporated now, including the Clyde, Oneida, Oswego, Mohawk, and Seneca rivers. The canal system was comprised of the new Erie Canal, the Cayuga-Seneca Canal between Cayuga and Seneca Lakes, the Oswego Canal from Syracuse to Oswego, and the Champlain Canal from Albany to Lake Champlain. It was called the New York State Barge Canal System when it opened in 1918.

The new canal system carried increasing amounts of traffic, but, eventually, efficient railroad freight traffic and truck traffic caused the demise of commercial use of the canal. In the late 1950s, the deathblow was applied by the completion of the New York State Thruway and the St. Lawrence Seaway, which linked the Great Lakes with the Atlantic Ocean.

◆ ◆ ◆

THREE CONFIGURATIONS OF THE ERIE CANAL

	Original Erie Canal	*Enlarged Erie Canal*	*Barge Canal-Erie Div.*
Year completed	1825	1862	1918
Length of canal	364 miles	350.5 miles	340.7 miles
Width of canal—top	40 ft	70 ft	123 ft (earth)
Width of the canal—bottom	28 ft	52-56 ft	75 ft (earth)
Depth of canal	4 ft	7 ft	12 ft
Size of locks	15 x 90 ft	18 x 110 ft	44.5 x 300 ft
Clearance under bridges	7.5 ft	11 ft	15.5 ft
Capacity of boats	75 tons	240-250 tons	2,000 tons
Size of boats	14 x 75 ft	16 x 96 ft	various

Notes on the Barge Canal-Erie Division (now renamed Erie Canal):

1. The rock sections are 94 feet wide and the river sections are 200 feet wide.
2. Except from the Hudson River to Oswego, the depth has been increased to 14 feet and the clearance to 20 feet.

Lock 32, Pittsford

• *chapter one* •

People of the Erie Canal

I've traveled all around this world and Tonawanda too,
I've been cast on desert island and beaten black and blue,
I fought and bled at Bull's Run, and wandered as a boy,
But I'll never forget the trip I took from Buffalo to Troy.

Whoa! Back! Get up!—Forget it I never shall,
When I drove a team of spavin mules on the E-ri-e Canal.

The cook we had on board the deck stood six feet in her socks;
Her hand was like an elephant's ear, and her breath would
open the locks.
A maid of fifty summers was she, the most of her body was on
the floor,
And when at night she went to bed, Oh sufferin'!
how she'd snore!

Whoa! Back! Get up! and tighten up your lines,
And watch the playful flies as on the mules they climb.
Whoa! Back! Duck your nut!—Forget I never shall,
When I drove a pair of spavin mules on the E-ri-e Canal.

– *Sung by Johnny Bartley at the "Alhambra Varieties" in Buffalo*

DEWITT CLINTON

DeWitt Clinton, the second son of James Clinton and Mary DeWitt Clinton, was born in Little Britain, Orange County, on March 2, 1769. DeWitt's father, James Clinton, was a Major General in the Continental Army and was second-in-command to Major General John Sullivan, who subdued the Iroquois Confederation in his campaign through the Finger Lakes Region in 1779.

In 1786, Clinton graduated first in his class from Columbia College. He studied law, was admitted to the bar, and was authorized to practice before the State Supreme Court. Upon completion of three years of legal training, he became private secretary to his uncle, George Clinton, who was the first Governor of New York. In 1797, he was elected to the State Assembly and the following year to a four-year term in the State Senate.

In February 1802, Clinton was appointed to finish John Armstrong's term in the U.S. Senate. He resigned in October 1803 to become mayor of the City of New York. With the exception of two years, the annual terms of 1807-08 and 1810-11, he was the mayor of New York from 1803 until 1815. As mayor, he was the organizer of the Public School Society, the patron of the New York Orphan Asylum, and the chief sponsor of the New York City Hospital. While serving as mayor, he also was a state senator from 1806 until 1811 and Lieutenant Governor from 1811 until 1813.

In 1815, when Clinton completed his last term as mayor, he devoted himself to promoting the project of building a state canal from the Great Lakes to the Hudson River. A short canal between the Mohawk River and Wood Creek had already been constructed, and the concept of additional canals had been discussed by Gouverneur Morris since 1803. Morris had reviewed his ideas with Simeon DeWitt, Clinton's cousin, who was Surveyor-General of the State of New York. Both men thought that it was feasible to build a canal across the State.

In 1807, Jesse Hawley of Canandaigua wrote and published a series of essays promoting the construction of a canal from Lake Erie to Utica on the Mohawk River. In 1808, state legislator Joshua Forman proposed that the Lake Erie canal route should be surveyed. The Surveyor-General commissioned James Geddes of Syracuse to do the actual surveying. Geddes also thought that it would be practical to build a canal across the state as far west as Lake Erie. Forman traveled to Washington, D.C., in an unsuccessful attempt to obtain federal funds for the New York canal project.

Clinton read all of the material about canals that he could find, including Hawley's essays and the history of European waterways. On March 13, 1810, both houses of the State Legislature voted for the formation of the Canal Commission and for an investigation of the practicality of a New York State canal. Clinton was one of the seven members of the Canal Commission.

In 1811, the members of the Canal Commission traveled along the prospective canal routes on horseback. Conditions were primitive, but they wanted to personally investigate the alternative routes. In 1812, Clinton made a strong but unsuccessful run for the presidency against James Madison on an independent ticket that attempted to strike a balance between the Democrats and the Federalists.

On June 3, 1817, the Canal Commission received bids for work on the canal and chose the contractors. That year, Clinton was nominated Governor of New York to succeed Daniel Tompkins who had been elected Vice President of the United States. On July 4, 1817, Clinton had the honor of digging the first spadeful of earth at Rome to initiate the construction of the middle section of the canal. Clinton retained the office of governor until 1822, when he lost the election to Robert Yates; he regained the office in 1824.

On April 12, 1824, as the result of maneuvering by his political opponents, Clinton was removed from his position on the Canal Commission. The maneuver backfired; the populace rebelled at the removal of the canal's stongest proponent from the commission. After all, the project was called "Clinton's Ditch."

In 1825, the Erie Canal was completed—about two years after its original scheduled completion date and approximately $2,000,000 over the original cost estimate. Those who had told Clinton that it would be an economic failure were wrong; it was a resounding economic success. On October 26, 1825, Governor DeWitt Clinton presided at the opening of the Erie Canal in ceremonies from Buffalo to New York. Clinton traveled the length of the canal on the leading canalboat, the *Seneca Chief*. The firing of cannons and the cheering of the crowds could be heard all along the route. Two barrels of water were transported from Lake Erie to New York to be poured into the Atlantic Ocean in a "wedding of the waters" ceremony.

Clinton's crowning achievement was sponsoring the construction of the Erie Canal. He was a naturalist and a man of many accomplishments, including serving as president of the American Academy of Art and the New York Historical Society and co-founding the Literary and Philosophical Society. He was also active in the Humane Society, the Lyceum of National History, and the Society for the Promotion of Useful Arts.

Clinton died an exhausted man on February 11, 1828, of a heart attack. In some respects, he had the ability to reach high national office. He was an honest, industrious man, but his personality prevented him from achieving his potential. He could be sarcastic and tactless, and he governed in a autocratic manner. Clinton was unwilling to share the powers of his office with strong lieutenants. He sneered at those who didn't share his vision of a waterway across the state to open up the Midwest and West. However, by any criteria, he achieved many goals and lived a life of accomplishment.

JAMES GEDDES

James Geddes was born on July 22, 1763, near Carlisle, Pennsylvania. In 1794, he moved to South Salina (now Syracuse), New York, and became one of the pioneers in the salt industry. The Onondaga County town of Geddes was named for him. He studied mathematics and law, was admitted to the bar, and in 1800 became a justice of the peace. In 1809, he was appointed judge of the county court and of the court of common pleas. He was elected to the State Assembly in 1804 and 1822 and served in the U.S. House of Representatives from 1813 to 1815.

During Geddes' first term in the State Assembly, Simeon DeWitt, the Surveyor-General of New York, discussed with him the possibility of a canal from the Great Lakes to the Hudson River. Geddes was initially interested in the idea because he envisioned the canal as a means of shipping salt economically from the salt springs to the Midwest. Later, he took a broader view of the potential of the canal for the economics of the region and of New York State. He visited other areas of the state to gather information and to promote interest in a canal.

In 1808, he conducted the first survey of a possible canal route at the request of Simeon DeWitt for a fee of $600. On January 20, 1809, he reported to the State Legislature that it would be possible to build a canal across the state. The route that Geddes proposed was essentially the one that was used. His report also included a survey of a canal route from Oneida Lake along the Oswego River to Lake Ontario.

Geddes was chosen as one of the four principal engineers to construct the Erie and Champlain Canals. Initially, he favored the use of inclined planes instead of locks to deal with the changes in elevation along the canal route. It was an impractical idea, and he wasn't one to stay with an idea that couldn't be made to work. From 1816 until 1822, he was assigned to the western division of the Erie Canal and then to the Champlain Canal.

In 1822, he surveyed a canal from the Ohio River to Lake Erie for the State of Ohio. In 1827, he examined routes for the Chesapeake and Ohio Canal for the federal government. In 1829, he investigated the feasibility of a canal route between the Tennessee and Alabama Rivers. Later he prepared a report for a canal from Sebago Lake to Westbrook in Maine. Geddes died on August 19, 1838, at Geddes, New York.

JESSE HAWLEY

Jesse Hawley, the oldest of eight children of Elijah Hawley and Mercy Bennett Hawley, was born on May 11, 1773, in Stratfield (now Bridgeport), Connecticut. In 1796, he moved to Canandaigua and worked as a clerk in the office of Oliver Phelps and Nathaniel Gorham, land developers. In 1803, he purchased a lot at the intersection of Main and Seneca Streets, Geneva, and entered into a partnership with Henry Corl. Hawley and Corl shipped flour for Colonel Mynderse's mills in Seneca Falls, ten miles east of Geneva.

The partners also shipped wheat on Durham boats via the Seneca River, Oneida Lake, Wood Creek, and the Western Inland Lock Navigation Company locks at Rome, Oneida County. Prior to the construction of canals, their route, which used natural waterways and overland turnpikes, followed the Mohawk River to Albany and then the Hudson River to the New York City market. The travel time was long and the cost of shipping was high. Hawley began to consider alternative routes to move flour and grain to market:

> *I first conceived the idea of the overland route of the canal, from Buffalo to Utica, in Col. Mynderse's office, in Seneca Falls, in 1805. I sat in a fit of abstraction for some minutes—then took down [Simeon] DeWitt's map of the State, spread it on the table and sat over it with my head reclined in my elbows on the table, ruminating over it, for—I cannot tell how long—muttering a head of water; at length my eye lit on the falls of Niagara, which instantly presented the idea that Lake Erie was that head of water.*

Hawley's friends, with whom he discussed his idea, considered his proposal to use water from Lake Erie for a canal across the state "a whimsical vagary."

In January, 1805, financial difficulties caused him to default on his mortgage payments on his Geneva property. Hawley's partner, Corl, declared bankruptcy and fled. According to the debtors' laws of New York, anyone who could not pay their debts would be jailed. In December, 1806, Hawley moved to Pittsburgh, Pennsylvania, to avoid jail, but he continued to think about a canal across New York State.

On January 14, 1807, the Pittsburgh *Commonwealth* published Hawley's essay in which he proposed a canal connecting Lake Erie with the Mohawk and Hudson Rivers. On July 12 of that year, he wrote a letter to Judge Erastus Granger in Buffalo,

New York, in which he described his proposed canal route and his optimistic opinion on the prospects for its completion.

During the summer of 1807, Hawley returned to Canandaigua to pay his debt to society and to begin a "prison limits" confinement of twenty months' duration. By "prison limits" was meant that the debtor was restricted to walking within a prescribed distance of the jail. This gave him an opportunity to reflect further on his idea for a canal. He wrote a series of fourteen essays entitled "Observation on Canals," which were published in Canandaigua's *Genesee Messenger.* Using the pen name "Hercules," he discussed many related canal topics, including:

- Benefits of Water Transportation
- Advantage to Inland Navigation by Canal
- Route Traced from Lake Erie to the Mohawk
- Resources of Capital
- Probable Size and Expense
- Other Improvements Proposed

Initially, Hawley proposed the construction of an inclined plane along much of the canal's route instead of using locks. After surveys were made of the western section of the canal route, this approach was proved to be impractical. His proposals for the building of a canal extending to Lake Erie were viewed as "the effusions of a maniac."

Jesse Hawley was not the only individual to consider improving existing waterways and building new and improved ones. Those who proposed improving internal navigation in the Province, later State, of New York, included Cadwallader D. Colden, Surveyor-General of the Province, in 1724; Sir Henry Moore, Governor of the Province, in 1768; Gouverneur Morris in 1777; and General George Washington in 1783.

Among those who proposed canals were Christopher Colles in 1784, Elkanah Watson in 1791, General Philip Schuyler in 1792, and Joshua Forman in 1807. Most of the early canal proposals included the use of Lake Ontario as the western section of the waterway. Gouverneur Morris is sometimes recognized as having, in 1803, the first idea for a continuous water-level canal from Lake Erie to the Hudson River.

After Hawley was released from prison, he became the deputy sheriff and jailer of Ontario county in 1809 and the assistant postmaster of Canandaigua in 1812. He moved to Rochester and, in 1817, was appointed Customs Collector for the Port of the Genesee River. He was elected secretary of the Monroe County Agricultural Society in 1821, and president of the Society in 1824. Also in 1821, he was elected to the State Assembly and acquired real estate holdings in Lockport near the canal. In 1822, he was elected the first supervisor of the town of Gates after the town of Greece was split off from it.

At the opening of the Erie Canal on October 26, 1825, Hawley was a member of the Rochester Canal Committee and traveled on the lead boat, *Seneca Chief,* with Governor DeWitt Clinton. Hawley was recognized for his part in publicizing the canal and gave a short address, which included the comment "In joining the Great Lakes with the Atlantic Ocean, New York made the longest canal—in the least time—with the least experience—for the least money—and of the greatest public utility of any other in the world."

In 1836, Hawley moved to Lockport to manage his real estate holdings in that area. He was elected treasurer of the village of Lockport, a position that he held until his death. He advocated enlarging the Erie Canal and spoke frequently on the subject. On May 11, 1835, the State Legislature passed the Erie Canal Act authorizing the expansion of the canal from a width of forty feet to seventy feet and from a depth of four feet to seven feet.

On July 4, 1840, Hawley wrote an essay about the Erie Canal:

> *No single act—no public measure—except the Declaration of Independence and the formation of the United States Constitution, has done so much to promote the public prosperity and produce a new era in the history of the country, as the construction of the Erie Canal.*

> *It is the father of canals in America; and of the State system of internal improvements which has grown up under its benign influences; and that its political influence and importance to the Union, for the construction of the internal improvements by State funds—as State properties—for State revenues, on the principle of State Rights is equal to its commercial value.*

The enlargement of the canal was completed in 1862 at a cost of over $32,000,000.

Hawley died on January 7, 1842, at Lockport. The white limestone shaft in Cold Springs Cemetery that serves as his headstone bears the words, "The subject of this memoir presented the first ideas of the Erie Canal as early as 1805 and continued its agitation until its completion about 1825. He advocated the enlargement of this great commercial artery and lived to see the work commenced." The City of Lockport changed the name of Bond Street to Hawley Street in his memory.

Although Gouverneur Morris is sometimes given credit for proposing the construction of the Erie Canal from the Hudson River to Lake Erie, Dorothie Bobbé observes in her *Life of DeWitt Clinton:* "Jesse Hawley it is who probably correctly stands first in advocating canal communications between Lake Erie and the Hudson River." In Hawley's own words, "I do not wish to be understood as saying that I was the first person or the only person who conceived the idea. I merely mean to say that with me it was a native thought, without having been suggested or communicated to me by any person, and that I was the first person who wrote and published articles."

GOUVERNEUR MORRIS

Gouverneur Morris, the only son of Lewis Morris and Sarah Gouverneur Morris, was born on January 31, 1752, in Morrisania, across the Harlem River from Manhattan. He graduated from King's College (now Columbia University) at the age of sixteen, studied law, and was admitted to the bar in 1771. In

1776-77, he served in the New York Provincial Congress and helped prepare the first draft of the State Constitution. In 1777-79, he served in the Continental Congress.

In 1779, after being defeated for re-election to the Continental Congress, Morris moved to Philadelphia, where he practiced law and published a series of essays on finance. While serving as assistant to Robert Morris, the U.S. Superintendent of Finance, from 1781 to 1785, Gouverneur prepared a report on coinage in which he suggested the use of the terms "dollar" and "cent." With modifications proposed by Thomas Jefferson, this plan was adopted as the basis of the U.S. coinage system. In 1787, Gouverneur Morris was one of Pennsylvania's representatives to the Constitutional Convention and was a member of the committee that drafted the final revision of the Constitution. In 1787, he returned to New York.

In 1789, Morris went to France on business and spent the next nine years abroad in France, England, Scotland, Germany, and Austria. The combination of having a brilliant mind, considerable self-assurance, social graces, and family influence preordained that Morris would choose a political career. In 1792, he was appointed U.S. Minister to France; he was the only representative of a foreign power who remained at his post during the Reign of Terror. In 1798, Morris returned to New York to practice law; he served as a U.S. Senator from 1800 to 1803.

Morris began to think about a canal across the state as early as 1777, when he discussed the idea with Philip Schuyler at Fort Edward. Beginning in 1801, Morris took an active interest in improving transportation between the Hudson River and Lake Erie. From 1810 until 1816, he was chairman of the seven-member New York State Board of Canal Commissioners, which prepared the plans for the Erie Canal. Morris was a visionary who observed, "As yet, we only crawl along the outer shell of our country. The interior excels the part we inhabit in soil, in climate, in everything. The proudest empire in Europe is but a bubble compared to what America will be, must be, in the course of two centuries, perhaps of one."

In 1811, Morris went to Washington, D.C., with DeWitt Clinton to request federal funds to build the Erie Canal. The

Madison administration was unwilling to provide any funds for the project. In fact, Madison's government was generally not known for providing aid for internal improvements. Clinton decided that New York State would have to proceed on its own, without federal support.

Morris was an enthusiastic supporter of the Erie Canal but not necessarily a practical one. He proposed that the canal be built on an inclined plane that began at Lake Erie and gradually dropped in elevation until it encountered the ridge near Albany. He envisioned using Lake Erie as a source of water to build "an artificial river directly across the country to the Hudson River."

At the time that Morris was proposing this approach, no survey of the western section had been made. Later, it became evident that this inclined plane would have been over 350 miles long and, in one location, would have been 150 feet above a valley. The sensible canal commissioners chose a plan that used locks to deal with the changes in elevation and aqueducts to lift the canal over river valleys.

Morris died on November 6, 1816, at the age of sixty-four. Although he was a patrician and was not a sponsor for the common man of the democracy, he never lost his joy of life. Just before his death, he wrote that he could still feel "the Gayety of Inexperience and the Frolic of Youth."

NATHAN ROBERTS

Nathan S. Roberts was born on July 28, 1776, at Piles Grove, New York. He was a self-educated mathematics teacher before becoming involved with the engineering of the Erie Canal. His early assignments on the canal included:

- surveying and locating, with Benjamin Wright of Rome, the section of the canal between Rome and Montezuma
- serving as Resident Engineer in charge of digging the canal between Rome and Syracuse in 1818
- locating the canal between the Seneca River and the village of Clyde in 1819
- planning the locks between Clyde and Rochester from 1819 until 1822

- locating and constructing the canal down the Clyde River and through the Cayuga marshes

The achievement for which he is most remembered is the engineering and construction from 1822 until 1825 of the locks at Lockport and of the canal between Lockport and Lake Erie. Roberts' challenge was to figure out how to raise the canal over the Niagara escarpment on its way west to Lake Erie. He reviewed the location of the locks recommended in the survey done by James Geddes and David Thomas and found that a depression in the escarpment to the east of the planned route was slightly lower; therefore, it was a better location for the locks since it would be easier and cheaper to get over the escarpment at that point.

In the spring of 1822, Roberts advertised for workers: "1,000 men wanted at Lockport—twelve dollars a month and "found" (room and board)." Immigrant workers flocked to Lockport to sign up. Their job was to dig and blast a two-mile-long channel through the seventy-five-foot-high face of the limestone escarpment. Fortunately, DuPont blasting powder was available to help them accomplish their task.

Blasters drilled holes in the limestone by hand and filled the holes almost full of blasting powder. They packed the powder down with clay and inserted fuses of twisted paper. Then they lit the fuses and ran. The work was extremely dangerous. The newly invented derricks that the workers used were flimsy and occasionally dropped stones on fellow workers below. A visiting journalist noted that the buildings of the village were protected from stone flying from the face of the escarpment after a blast "by trunks of trees, about six inches at the butt, and long enough when set around the buildings at about 45 degrees, to meet at the top."

Roberts' design for the locks was his most significant achievement. His design included two sets of five locks each, one set for westbound traffic up the escarpment and one set for eastbound traffic down the escarpment. Each of the five locks in a set lifted (or lowered) a boat twelve feet vertically, nearly fifty percent more than the locks used elsewhere on the canal. One of the purposes of the locks was to admit water from Lake Erie into the canal system. In the early going, the work was difficult and risky; schedules were not being met. Additional workers had to be hired and soon "two thousand Irishmen were working night and day."

The locks at Lockport were considered to be one of the greatest engineering accomplishments in America up to that time. Roberts became known as the "Father of the Lockport Five." After the completion of the Erie Canal in 1825, Roberts was appointed Chief Engineer of the canal from Pittsburgh to Kaskiminetas in Pennsylvania and of the Pennsylvania Canal. In 1828, he was appointed a member of the Board of Engineers of the Chesapeake and Ohio Canal Company. He designed and built the bridge across the Potomac River at Harpers Ferry.

From 1830 to 1832, Roberts worked for the federal government as Chief Engineer in charge of a study to build a ship canal around Muscle Shoals on the Tennessee River in Alabama. From 1835 until 1841, he worked as Chief Engineer with John B. Jervis and Holmes Hutchison on the enlargement of the Erie Canal. Roberts died on November 24, 1852, at Lenox, Madison County, New York.

Canvass White

Canvass White, the second son of Hugh White, Jr., and Tryphena Lawrence White, was born September 8, 1790, in Whitestown, Madison County. He attended Fairfield Academy, worked in a local store, and, for health reasons, traveled to Russia on a merchant vessel. He served in the army during the War of 1812 and was wounded during the capture of Fort Erie.

In 1816, White assisted Benjamin Wright in making the early surveys of the Erie Canal. The following year White asked DeWitt Clinton and Benjamin Wright to authorize him to go to England, at his own expense, to investigate that country's many canals. His goal was to learn as much as he could to apply to the building of the Erie Canal. In early 1818, he wrote to his father that, on foot, he had "traveled 400 miles, passed through a number of tunnels and over several aqueducts. One aqueduct ... consists of nineteen arches of cast iron." Before he returned to the

United States, he had traveled 2,000 miles along England's and continental Europe's canals.

Upon his return home, White found that the construction cost of locks on the canal was considerably higher than the estimates. One reason for the cost overruns was the cost of hydraulic cement, which had to be imported from Europe. White heard that Mason Harris of Chittenango, Madison County, was using a type of limestone in his aqueducts and culverts between Rome and Syracuse that could withstand water pressure. The cement that Harris made from this limestone wouldn't "slack"; that is, it wouldn't become diluted or weaken in contact with water. White found that this particular type of limestone hardened when put into water.

White conducted experiments with this limestone. He mined it, analyzed its properties, and experimented with a variety of proportions in mixing the ingredients, which were sand and limestone that had been pulverized and burned. In fact, White "invented" New York's own version of hydraulic cement. Dr. Barto of Herkimer noted that White's cement was "not inferior to the Roman [cement] of Puteoli or the Dutch Tarras of the Rhine."

White was granted a patent for his waterproof cement on February 1, 1820. The use of this cement improved the quality and significantly reduced the cost of culverts and locks on the canal. Benjamin Wright said that White's invention gave "an incalculable benefit to the State."

White worked on the Erie Canal for nine years and held responsible positions on the eastern segment, including the supervision of the Glens Falls feeder. Upon completion of the Erie Canal in 1825, he became Chief Engineer of the Union Canal in Pennsylvania. Subsequently, he was a consulting engineer for the Farmington Canal, the Schuylkill Navigation Company, and for the Windsor locks on the Connecticut River. Also, he was Chief Engineer for Delaware and Raritan Canal in New Jersey and the Lehigh Canal in Pennsylvania. White, whose health had never been good, died at the relatively young age of forty-four in late 1834 in St. Augustine, Florida.

BENJAMIN WRIGHT

Benjamin Wright, the son of Ebenezer Wright and Grace Butler Wright, was born on October 10, 1770, in Wethersfield, Connecticut. He studied law, mathematics, and surveying to take advantage of the opportunity for those "capable of surveying and preparing deeds" in the newly settled Mohawk Valley in New York. Wright and his parents moved to Fort Stanwix, now Rome, New York, in 1789. In 1791, he assisted with the survey for a canal to join the Mohawk River and Wood Creek near Rome, the first survey for a canal in New York State. From 1792 until 1796, he made land surveys of over 50,000 acres in Oneida and Oswego counties.

This region became one of the important agricultural areas of the state, and Wright developed an interest in transporting crops to market. Since the roads of that time were little more than trails, he became interested in canals. In 1792, the English engineer William Weston completed canal construction near Little Falls on the Mohawk River for the Western Inland Lock and Navigation Company. When Weston returned to England, Wright conducted surveys of Wood Creek and of the Mohawk River to Schenectady for the Western Inland Navigation Company. However, the company lacked the financial resources to proceed with their plans.

Wright became a leader of the Rome community. He was routinely elected to the State Legislature and was appointed a county judge. In 1811, he examined a proposed canal route from Rome on the Mohawk River to Waterford on the Hudson River for the State Canal Commission, and the following year he examined a route from Seneca Lake to Rome. In early 1816, the State Canal Commission was reorganized, and the responsibility of canal construction was given to Wright and to James Geddes of Syracuse.

Later that year when the law was enacted to proceed with the Erie Canal, Geddes was given the responsibility for the western portion, Wright the middle section from Rome to Seneca Lake, and Charles C. Broadhead the eastern segment. On July 4, 1817, the construction of the canal was begun at Rome. Wright directed crews of workmen to set five rows of red markers to mark the path of the canal. The middle row marked the center of the canal, the inside rows forty feet apart next to the middle row noted the width of the canal, and the outside rows sixty feet apart marked the limits of the land to be cleared. Next crews of borers dug holes twelve feet deep to investigate excavating conditions for the construction crews.

Subsequently, David Thomas took over the responsibility for the western section from Geddes, who shifted to work on the Champlain Canal. The section of the Erie Canal near Rome was opened in late 1819, and a flat-bottomed boat named the *Chief Engineer of Rome* in honor of Benjamin Wright traveled on the canal. The portion of the canal as far west as Brockport was finished in 1823, and the entire canal was completed in 1825.

Wright was known not only for his abilities as a surveyor and his knowledge of construction, but also for his managerial ability. He selected a capable group of young men to work for him, including not only Nathan Roberts and Canvass White, but also John B. Jervis, who became the foremost American civil engineer prior to the Civil War, and David Stanhope Bates, who was responsible for the crossing of the Erie Canal over the Irondequoit Valley and the Genesee River at Rochester.

No formal schools of Civil Engineering existed at the time that the Erie Canal was built. The planning and construction of the canal was the country's engineering school in the early nineteenth century, and Wright became known as the "Father of American Engineering."

From 1821 to 1827, Wright served as consulting engineer on the Blackstone Canal in Rhode Island, the Chesapeake and Delaware Canal, the Delaware and Hudson Canal (which was completed by John Jervis), and the Farmington Canal in Connecticut. From 1828 to 1831, he was Chief Engineer of the Chesapeake and Ohio Canal, and he was Chief Engineer of the St. Lawrence Ship Canal in 1833. In 1837, he was a consulting engineer for a canal from Chicago to the Illinois River and also for the Welland Canal. Wright died on August 24, 1842.

◆ ◆ ◆

Canalboat, Erie Canal Museum, Syracuse

Packett's Landing, Fairport

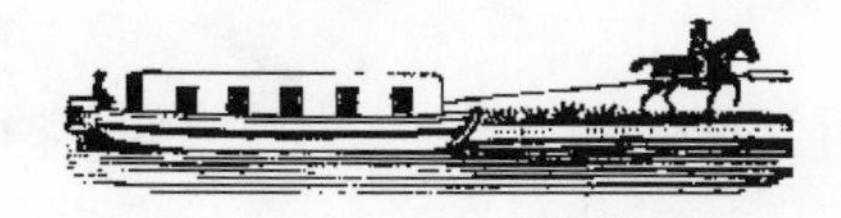

• chapter two •

Erie Canal Stories

We are cutting a Ditch through the gravel,
Through the gravel across the state, by heck!
We are cutting the Ditch through the gravel,
So the people and the freight can travel,
Can travel across the state, by heck!

We are digging the Ditch through the mire;
Through the mud and the slime and the mire, by heck!
And the mud is our principal hire;
In our pants, up our sleeves, down our neck, by heck!
The mud is our principal hire.

We are cutting the Ditch through the rocks,
Through the rocks across the state, by heck!
We are cutting the Ditch through the rocks,
And we'll finish her off with stone locks,
From the rocks across the state, by heck!
From the rocks across the state.

Anonymous

LIFE ON THE CANAL

In the early days of the Erie Canal, the arrival of a luxury canal packet was a high point in the lives of those who lived along the canal. It brought drama and a view of the outside world into their lives. The first blast of the packet horn brought a rush of people to the wharf to watch the matched pairs of horses with their expensive harnesses. The captain was permitted to shorten his towline and move to the favored inner lane of the towpath as he passed by the towlines of all other waiting boats at a rate of four miles per hour.

The packet brought mail, newspapers, and large quantities of gossip and rumors. Ladies holding frilled parasols to protect themselves from the sun's rays sat on low-backed benches on the deck. Their bustles were positioned to stand out at the proper angle, and draped skirts modestly covered their ankles. The gentlemen lounged about the deck in tailored pearl-gray coats, tapered trousers, and ruffled white shirts that earned them the name "ruffleshirts."

Many of the travelers were from Europe, but central and western New York were almost as foreign to the Easterners as they were to the Europeans. The passengers found much that measured up to their expectations: the serenity of the forests, fabulous views from the high aqueducts over the rivers, and the experience of passing through the locks. The five-step locks in both directions at Lockport were particularly impressive.

Travelers saw a variety of birds and animals that appeared to be tame as they stopped to watch the packet pass by. The silent movement of the boat was a pleasant change from the bumpy stagecoach ride from Albany to Schenectady. The only disruption in their otherwise uneventful ride was the occasional cry of "Low bridge—everybody down." In order to humor farmers whose property was split by the canal, the state had promised them bridges across the canal for easy access to both parcels of their land. Then, to save money, the bridges were built low. More than one passenger failed to respond to the low bridge warning in time and was scraped off the top deck.

As pleasant as the journey was to them initially, not all passengers considered it pleasant after they had been aboard for awhile. Insects, particularly mosquitoes, caused considerable discomfort. Ladies wore veils and continually fanned themselves, and gentlemen wore cloaks even in hot, humid weather. Another problem, once canal transportation became popular, was overcrowding. The packets were not designed for the number of passengers that were booked.

Each evening after dinner, crewmen began to convert the dining saloon into sleeping quarters by pushing the benches and tables into the center of the compartment. They installed three or four rows of twelve-inch-wide shelves along the bulkheads that were suspended by chains or ropes from the overhead. The top shelf was only eight inches from the overhead. A crewman then placed a thin pallet, a sheet, and a thin blanket on each shelf. Passengers for whom there were no shelves were placed on benches or tables, or slept under a table. On the fancier packets, a curtain was pulled across the forward section of the dining saloon to give the ladies an illusion of privacy. Obviously, every sound could be heard through the curtain.

The ladies took off their hats and shoes and loosened their corsets; the gentlemen removed their boots, coats, and hats. Few passengers made any attempt to undress to get ready for bed. They bumped their heads on the next higher shelf if they attempted to raise them, and they could not turn over without falling off the shelf. A passenger would be laughed at if he had a problem getting onto his assigned shelf, particularly a heavy man who attempted to climb into a top shelf.

Charles Dickens traveled on an Erie Canal packet boat. He explained how he dealt with the problem of snug sleeping quarters: "My shelf being a bottom one, I finally determined on lying on the floor, gently rolling in, stopping immediately I touched the mattress, and remaining for the night with that side uppermost, whatever it might be. Luckily, I came upon my back at exactly the right moment."

The passengers did not sleep in silence. Frequently, the captain would blow the boat's horn to pass slower boats, particularly cargo boats, and the crew could be heard walking around the deck immediately overhead. With little air circulation, the sleeping quarters became stifling, and the sound of snoring could be heard in many keys.

Early in the morning, all passengers were turned out of the dining saloon to permit the crew to get it ready for breakfast. Then the unrefreshed passengers could stand in line on the deck to wash their faces in wash basins filled with cloudy canal water. One consolation was the food on the packets, which was usually good and plentiful. For breakfast, the cook frequently prepared fried fish and meat, fresh bread, butter, honey and maple syrup, assorted pickles, puddings, and steaming pitchers of tea. The other two meals of the day usually consisted of roast meat and game, fresh vegetables, and a wide choice of cakes and pies.

Some passengers became bored with the trip. Long periods of waiting were common at the locks and while picking up or leaving off passengers or loading or offloading supplies at village wharves. Ladies could shop at the canalside stores or stroll through the village, but their options were limited. Gentlemen had more options: playing games of chance at carnival booths, visiting a circus boat, or betting on a variety of spectacles such as fistfights. Many professional gamblers, pretending to be wealthy Easterners with business in the West, traveled on the packets. While waiting at a lock or a wharf, they would casually suggest a game of cards. Using marked cards, they relieved many unwary travelers of their excess cash.

Concerned with the widespread drinking and gambling along the canal, missionary ministers rode the packets to spread their message to a captive audience. Most captains allowed them to conduct prayer meetings in the dining saloons. At one point, the missionaries had persuaded the State not to allow travel on the canal on Sundays. Eventually the economic advantage of working a seven-day week prevailed.

However, conditions were quite different on a canal freighter, which was usually the floating home for the captain and his family. The captain's wife had a small compartment in the stern that she decorated as her house. Usually curtains brightened the inside of the windows, and flower pots decorated the outside. The family compartment was too small to accommodate a cooking stove, so the stove was placed on the rear deck. No roof covered the stove; an umbrella made it possible to cook in the rain. Clothes were washed in the canal and dried on lines rigged over the cargo.

Either the captain and his wife operated the boat or a person was hired to assist the captain. The captain and his wife or helper took turns steering. Sleep had to be caught in snatches while waiting at a lock or a wharf. The children usually served as "hoggees" controlling the teams of horses or mules on the tow-path. Cargo boats moved at an average speed of one and a half miles per hour. The canal was an inexpensive way to move cargo but not a fast way.

The economics of canal travel were very favorable both for passenger and freight traffic. However, as more and more rail-roads were built, the canal system had increasing difficulty in competing for business. Geography was ultimately against the canals because cargo had to be offloaded and reloaded to other means of transportation for distribution.

A LITTLE WHITE LIE

Perry Joslin was the lock-tender at a very remote and sparsely settled section of the Erie Canal. People considered Perry to be daffy, but then maybe all lock-tenders were a little touched. They spent much of their time alone, and they didn't seem to mind the strong winds that blew along the canal in the early spring and late fall. In the late 1860s, the only people with whom Perry talked were the canallers traveling west to Buffalo and east to Albany. His small lock-tender's house stood adjacent to the lock overlooking the valley. No other house could be seen from his windows.

A plank road ran parallel to the canal. For much of the length of that section of the canal, the road was visible from the canal. However, at Perry's lock, the road was uphill from the canal and was hidden by trees. Perry could hear the wagons passing by, but they were too far away for him to be able to talk with the drivers and passengers.

Perry was tall and thin and had a look of clumsiness about him. His long shoulder-length white hair was usually covered with a floppy hat, and his shirttail hung out more than it stayed tucked in. He had small facial features and a weak chin. The wind blowing down the canal made his eyes water, and his gloveless hands were always chapped in colder weather.

One early March, the first canal boat from the east was the *Young Lion*, an old yellow-green bullhead boat. Three boats had already passed through the lock heading east, but Perry didn't consider the lock to be officially open until the first boat traveling west arrived. The *Young Lion's* captain, Esau Brown, and her driver, John, were one of the most efficient teams on the canal and could also hold their own in a fight.

Celia Brown immigrated to the United States from England and worked as a lady's maid in Utica until she met Lucy Cashdollar. Lucy operated the Agency for Bachelor Boaters out of Bentley's Bar and provided cooks for unmarried canalboat captains. Celia had hired on with Esau as his cook, and they were married within a year. Perry liked the way that Celia had decorated the living quarters on the boat. He wished that he had bright yellow curtains in his windows.

Celia invited Perry on board for a cup of tea and expressed her sympathy on the death of his mother. The woman wasn't Perry's natural mother. She had followed a band of Gypsies along the plank road until she arrived at Perry's lock. She adopted him, called herself his mother, and took charge of his lock-house and his wages. Part of his wages went for her drinks at a distant village. She beat him occasionally, and, initially, he wished that she would go away. However, he missed her and was more lonely than ever since she died.

Celia Brown suggested to Perry that he get married, so that he wouldn't be so lonely at his quiet outpost. As he watched the stern of the *Young Lion* moving up the canal, he wondered if he should take Celia's advice. He didn't really know how to find a bride. He was considered a strange fellow. A boater would say, "There's Perry. He's the queerest coot on the whole canal." Perry would shake his head in agreement and say, "That's right, I guess." He had never been loved and never been in love. He wondered what it would be like to be in love. He had watched couples kissing on the decks on the canal boats but had never experienced it himself.

The lock house was sparsely furnished. The State provided a table, three chairs, and a built-in bunk bed. He used to sleep in the loft room, but he brought his blankets downstairs where he slept on straw provided by boaters. After the *Young Lion* left, he baked some beans for supper and thought some more about Celia's suggestion that he get married. Then he read for a while. He read the Bible and Dicken's *Old Curiosity Shop,* the only books that he had, over and over.

With the beginning of the spring weather in April, Perry was moody. His missed the old woman's company and was increasingly lonely. He frequently thought about Celia Brown's advice to get married. When the paywagon came to Perry's lock at the end of April, they told him that in two weeks the canal was going to be closed for three days for repairs. Maintenance men were going to patch a culvert and replace the planking in a aqueduct over a brook. When Perry told one of the maintenance men that he was going to look for a wife, the man suggested that Perry should use this time to do his sparking.

The evening before the canal was to be closed, Perry pressed his pants, darned his socks, and shined his shoes. The next morning he put on his best blue flannel shirt and donned his old black coat with its swallow-tail lapels. He strolled down into the valley and crossed the footbridge that led up to Potato Hill. The muddy water came within an inch of the bridge. He had to use his hands to climb the hill, and he began to perspire and grow tired.

Perry walked slowly, enjoying the bloom of spring all around him. The ground was still wet from the spring rains, and he could see ferns, the leaves of dogtooth violets, cup-like anemones in many colors, and wild leeks growing at the edge of the woods. He watched a blue jay drinking from a stream and realized that he was no longer tired. He walked up a muddy path that led to a house with a large barn behind it. The house and barn were in need of paint, and the farm looked run down.

Chickens pecked and scratched in a garden patch, ducks marched through the puddles, and a black and white dog barked once in greeting. An old goose honked at him and waddled into the barn. A cat was asleep on the porch, two young boys were playing in the yard, and a woman was hanging wash on the line. Perry stopped to talk with the woman, who looked tired and old before her time. She said that her husband was buying supplies in the village, and that Perry was welcome to eat his lunch in the barn. Perry entered the barn and walked along a row of stanchions to a pile of hay. Broken tools stacked along the wall and the general state of disrepair verified that this was a poor farm.

Perry sat down in the pile of hay and began to eat his lunch before he heard the girl sitting in the shadow next to him. Perry greeted her, and she replied, "Hello, mister" in a soft, blurred voice. He offered her some of his cheese. She stood, walked over to him until he thought she was going to step on him, and asked what his name was. He told her it was Perry Joslin. He placed the cheese in her hands, and she squatted in front of him. She had long black hair and the most beautiful brown eyes that he had ever seen. She wore a faded gingham dress and her legs were well-muscled from working around the farm.

She asked, "What do you look like, mister?" Perry moved backward and asked, "Why?" He noted that her eyes looked beyond him but appeared to focus on his lips each time that he spoke. She said, "I'm blind." Then she asked if she could feel his face, and he said,"Surely." Her fingers had a light touch but showed no hesitation. He looked at her as her fingers moved like small, hovering moths on his face. He felt very peaceful, and deep down he felt a gladness. She was the most beautiful thing that he had ever seen. Her hands had the smell of the earth and woods, and he was reminded of the beauty of the forest during his walk to the farm.

She asked what color his eyes were, and he replied, "Blue." She asked, "How old are you, mister?" He said that he didn't know, and she told him that she was seventeen. He noted that she was a big girl for her age. She asked what color his long hair was, and he replied, "Gold." She asked, "Pure gold?" He had not meant to respond that way, but somehow he didn't want to tell her that his hair was gray. She asked if gold was like the yellow in buttercups, and he said that it was.

Perry asked her if she had been born blind. She said that she could remember seeing, but that she had lost her sight during an illness. When he asked what she did around the farm, she replied that she milked the cows and took care of the ducks and hens. He inquired how she found the animals; she replied that instead of going to them she called them to her. She told him that she talked to the animals, and that they came to her when she called. To demonstrate, she called the old goose by making a odd noise with her lips. The goose came to her and rubbed against her arm.

Perry asked her what her name was. She replied, "Eve. Eve Winslow. They call me blind Eve." He asked, "Are you happy, Eve?" She responded, "Sometimes." She asked him where he was going, and he told her he was going sparking. She asked what that meant. He answered that he was looking for a girl to live with him. She inquired where he lived, and he told her that he tended a lock on the canal and lived in a two-room house with one room on the first floor and the other one above it.

Eve asked what the canal was and was told that it was a channel of water used for both passenger and cargo boats. Perry described how the boats blow a horn to call him to let the water out of the lock and lower the boat to the next level. She asked if he could hear the wind from his house, and he acknowledged that you could because it stood on the edge of the valley. With her eyes shining, Eve said, "Oh, mister, I would like to live there."

He described the lock-tender's shack to her. They shared the tart that he had brought with him, and they talked some more. Occasionally, she would reach over and rub his hair. He asked if she would like to come and live with him; she replied, "Oh, yes." Perry realized that he wasn't offering much, but he was talking with someone worse off than he was. Perry told Eve that he would speak to her father, and that they would get married.

Eve told him that she didn't have a dress to wear to the wedding. Perry offered to bring one for her. When she stood up, she had a mature figure and was as tall as he was but broader in the shoulders. Perry put his arm around her and kissed her. It was the first kiss for both of them, and initially she was tense. Her lips felt moist and tight; they loosened, and she began to shiver. His ears tingled, and his voice wavered. He took her hand as they went to tell her mother and to wait for her father to return.

Her mother admitted that she didn't think that Eve would ever marry. She thought that her husband would readily agree to the marriage. When Eve's father returned from the village, he agreed to the union and spoke kindly of his daughter. He told Perry that she would make a good wife. The wedding date was set for two weeks hence, and Perry made arrangements to take Eve to the village to save Mr. Winslow the cost of bringing the minister to his home.

Perry gave Eve a good-bye kiss and walked home a happy man. He had completed his sparking and hadn't even made it to the top of Potato Hill. He kept remembering Eve saying, "Oh, yes," and her warm, trembling kiss. When he awoke the next morning, he counted his money. He calculated that after buying the marriage license and some things for the house, such as extra blankets, that he would have about five dollars left.

When the canal reopened two days later, the boaters asked him what he had done on his three days off. When he told them that he had been sparking, they all laughed at him and asked what she looked like. He told them that she was seventeen, was as tall as he was, and had long black hair. He added that she was beautiful. They asked Perry why she would have him as her husband. He said that he didn't know, but that he thought she liked his hair. That made the boaters laugh, so he stopped commenting on it. He didn't want them to tell Eve that his hair was gray.

When the *Young Lion* returned from the West, Esau offered to tend the lock for two days when Perry and Eve were married. John the driver told Perry that if the boaters gave him a hard time to let him know. Celia Brown offered to buy the extra blankets for the shanty. Esau reminded Perry to get the license early. As the wedding day approached, the boaters kidded Perry mercilessly. One boater gave him a wedding gift of an umbrella to shield his golden hair from the sun. That story traveled the length of the canal.

Perry traveled to the village to buy a suit, a wedding dress, and a wedding ring. This left him with enough to pay the minister. The minister was a tall, sad man, but Perry seemed to make him smile. Perry returned to the Winslow farm, where the goose honked at him again as he went to sleep in the hay. He awoke the next morning to find Eve stroking his hair. He untied his package and gave Eve her dress. She explored it with her fingertips and ran into the house to try it on.

Eve's mother helped her dress and bound her hair in a ribbon. Perry and Eve had breakfast with the Winslows. Eve's father was in a jovial mood, but her mother had tears in her eyes. After breakfast, the couple walked to the village. The words of the wedding ceremony rang in Perry's ear as they walked hand in hand from the village to the lock. They stopped in a meadow and had supper from a bag that Perry had brought with him. Occasionally, Eve raised her finger to her mouth and put her tongue on her ring. She asked Perry what color it was; he replied, "gold," and she ran her fingers through his hair.

As they approached the shanty, Perry could see the bow lantern of the *Young Lion*. A light glowed in the window of the shack and Celia Brown got up from her chair to greet them as they entered. The Browns and John had bought wedding presents for the newlyweds: an oil lamp, a rocking chair, a set of crockery, and bright blue window curtains. As Celia took Eve's hand and kissed her, the older woman's eyes moistened. When Esau and John came into the house, Perry could see that they also thought that Eve was beautiful. Celia told Eve, "Perry is a good man, dearie. And your house is the pleasantest one in the world. I know. I've been here two days now." The Browns and John left the house with good wishes to Eve and Perry, and the two men locked the *Young Lion* through. Wherever they went, the canalers had already heard the story of Perry's golden hair.

Eve and Perry were married for many years. The boatmen tried to tell her that Perry's hair wasn't gold, but she just pointed to her ring in response. Occasionally, one of the canalers would make advances toward her, but she was strong and never had to call upon Esau and John for help. Eve learned her way around the house by touch and became a good cook. She was good with the horses and mules pulling the canal boats and prevented the use of the whip to spur the animals on many occasions. She was as sure of herself on the plank across the lock as Perry was. Everyone enjoyed listening to her singing in the evening. She was in love with Perry until he died. When he passed away, she cut off a lock of his golden hair to remember him by.

The Montezuma Mosquitoes

The northern end of Cayuga Lake is a vast marsh. In the 1820s, it was called the Cayuga Marshes or Nine Mile Swamp; today it is the Montezuma National Wildlife Refuge. The Cayuga Indians warned the first surveyors who came to the marshes about the mosquitoes and the illness that they brought. Local laborers were reluctant to work in the marshes. However, the Irish laborers were willing to take on the challenge. They were afraid of snakes but not mosquitoes.

The Seneca River, which drained into the marshes, presented a serious problem to canal engineers. In a dry spell, the river was three feet below the level of the swamp; during the spring rains, it was two feet above it. The laborers began to dig in the swamp in May, but high water from the Seneca River prevented them from working on the eleven-mile section between Montezuma and Clyde. The teams sat around in their bunk houses for three weeks until the level of the river went down. In June, digging began in earnest.

At first, the job looked easy. There were no rocks to contend with, the dirt was soft, and the workers could excavate the canal rapidly. The problem was that it wouldn't stay dug. When they returned the next morning, the banks had turned to mud and had slid back into the excavation. The laborers made pilings of stakes in these soft spots along the canal's path and used planks across the pilings to hold the moist dirt in place.

The contractors counted on a layer of marl—a mixture of clay, the remnants of shells, and small stones—under the slush of the marsh to receive the stakes that they drove in to build the pilings. However, about one in twenty of the stakes vanished into the quicksand into which it was being driven.

The Irish workers were used to working in quicksand, but standing in water above their knees all day made their legs swell and become a prime target for leeches. Laborers worked shirtless and suffered from sunburn. Irish laborers gave names to the sections that gave them the most trouble: "Breakback Bog," "Bottomless Pit," "Digger's Misery," and "Mud-turtles' Delight."

The mosquitoes came late in 1821. Usually, they were out in large quantities by early June. They didn't come until mid-July, but when they came they arrived in great numbers. The workers' hands became so swollen that they could hardly hold their tools; their eyes swelled until they were almost shut. The digging of the canal slowed down. Men hung smudge-buckets around their necks. Smudge-buckets, called "Montezuma necklaces," were small pails stuffed with damp leaves and twigs covering a slow fire. The rising smoke probably kept away some of the mosquitoes; it also caused raw noses, red eyes, and much coughing.

By mid-August, fever had broken out. Many laborers developed the "shakes" and were unable to work. Half of the men couldn't get up for breakfast and begin work. Many panicked and left their jobs, if they could walk.

On August 15, one contractor advertised for replacements: "Two hundred men wanted at once for the Cayuga Marshes. No wet feet. No disease. Top pay." A contractor's agent posted notices at the Exchange Hotel in Auburn: "Wanted; men ... Pleasant work ... Tavern-style Keep ... High Wages." He told the men: "Seven shillings a day, boys ... A dollar after two months ... Tavern prog ... Medical Care free ... Whiskey every night if you get the shakes." He found no takers.

Doctors thought that malaria was breathed in. After all, the word meant "bad air." They treated their fever patients the same way they treated patients for other illnesses; they bled them. After bleeding their patients, doctors gave them feverwort, green pigweed, snake-root, and Seneca Oil (kerosene). They also experimented with "Jesuits' bark" from Peru, with which they had good results since it was an early form of quinine.

Eventually, as the summer progressed and the cool weather of autumn arrived, the mosquitoes ceased to be a problem and the men returned to work. What appeared to be a major threat to the completion of DeWitt Clinton's plans for a canal across the state was overcome and work continued.

PILKINGTON'S FOUR-SKATE ESCAPADE

One evening in late November, 1893, Grandfather Adams was visited by his grandsons. Winter had come early that year, but by Thanksgiving the temperature had risen, turning the ice on the Erie Canal to slush. The young men had been skating on the canal every day, and they were disappointed at this break in the winter. They complained to their grandfather about this lapse in their daily outings. After listening to their moaning about being inactive, he offered to tell them a skating story.

Grandfather Adams was a young man during the winter of 1826 when he had gone to Owego representating the Wayne County Horse-Thief Society to investigate the loss of New York State horses across the Pennsylvania border. Young Adams and his friend and college classmate, Lathrop, stayed at an inn on the Susquehanna River in the town of Tioga.

The town was enjoying a winter carnival on the river, and the two visitors were invited to join in the activities. The young men, who had brought their ice skates with them, walked down to the bonfire on the riverbank. The fire lighted the scene of men and women gliding on the smooth ice and enjoying the festivities. Over the embers of fire was hung a large cast iron kettle that heated water to prepare hot buttered rum for taking the edge off the cold winter evening.

Maurice, who owned the local iron works and was a Justice of the Peace, greeted them and invited them to join in the fun with his friends and neighbors. Adams was a teetotaler, but Lathrop decided to live up to his college reputation as a man who could hold his drinks. After several hot buttered rums, he began to extol the skating ability of his friend, Adams, and to play down the talent of the local skaters. Young Lathrop claimed that his friend was the finest skater in the state.

Adams protested that his abilities were being overstated, but the crowd couldn't be convinced. They demanded that he display his aptitude on the ice. While the reluctant skater was strapping on his skates, Lathrop talked further about his friend's talent, making the claim that he was the ice skating champion of the Erie Canal and nearby bodies of water. Resolved to do his best to live up to his billing, Adams skated well and was cheered on by the crowd from the southern tier of New York State and the northern tier of Pennsylvania. Finally, urged on by the crowd, he made some daring moves that broke a strap on his skates, which caused a nasty fall.

Adams rested by the fire while he repaired his skate strap. The crowd's praise was almost universal. When the accolades began to die down, a loud jeer was heard from a nearby graveyard. The man sitting on the graveyard fence who had given the "Bronx cheer" climbed down from the fence and walked toward the crowd. He was short and powerfully built with a wild look on his face. The stranger had long arms, bowed legs, and high cheekbones. He was dressed in dark, worn clothing that contributed to his simian appearance.

He introduced himself as Solomon Silliman and was offered a tot of hot buttered rum by Maurice, who asked the man what had brought him here. He said that he was walking through the area and had stopped to watch the youngster's amateur skating exhibition. Lathrop asked the stranger if he thought that he could skate better. He replied that he could perform better with a skillet strapped to one foot and his grandmother's flatiron strapped to the other. Lathrop turned to the gathering and asked if someone would loan this braggart a pair of skates.

A local merchant named Saunders offered to loan the stranger his skates. Silliman strapped them on, tested the ice, and told the crowd that he would start with a simple exercise. He skated fast across the river and then back toward the gathering, shifting back and forth from the inner edge of the blades to the outer edge with ease. Every movement showed that he was, indeed, an expert skater. He performed a series of figures, the Fairy Float, the Double Buck and Wing, the Dutchman's Delight, the Dying Hawk, and the Rat-tat-too. He finished his demonstration by standing on the points of the skates and doing the Rutland Wiggle, a popular but vulgar dance step.

The crowd cheered as he returned to the bonfire for another drink of hot buttered rum. They demanded that he continue with his performance. He tightened the straps on his skates and asked for another pair of skates. Saunders the merchant asked what was wrong with his. Silliman said that they were fine, but that one pair of skates wasn't enough for a skater of his ability. He walked up to the town baker and asked him to take off his skates. The baker asked him if he was going to take off the pair that he had on first. Silliman said that he wasn't because he was going to wear the baker's pair on his hands. The baker reluctantly removed his skates and handed them to Silliman.

Silliman looked at the skates and shook his head. He went over to the sandbank along the river's edge and picked out several large chunks, which he broke into loose sand to rub on the edges of the skates. Then he filled his pockets with the loose sand, explaining that it was required to help him maintain balance in the complicated maneuvers that he was going to demonstrate. The baker helped Silliman strap the skates to his hands.

Silliman announced to the crowd that he was known as Four-Skate Pilkington in Europe, where he had performed for royalty. He explained that he would start by skating upriver and then return skating hand and foot, foot and hand, to demonstrate skating on all fours. As he was making this announcement, a horse on the nearby turnpike neighed in distress, and several men left to investigate. Because of the recent thefts of horses in the vicinity, Maurice became suspicious of Silliman and was determined to question him upon his return.

Silliman's speed increased when he was thirty yards away, and, by the time he was sixty yards downstream, he was racing for the bend in the river a half mile away. By the light of the moon, the crown could see him shake off the skates from his hands and to move them in circling movements as though he were sowing seed. When it became clear that Four-Skate, now Two-Skate, Pilkington was not coming back, Maurice called out to the other men to help in the chase. Saunders the merchant bemoaned the fact that he wasn't going to see his skates again.

Adams, Lathrop, Maurice, and the Methodist minister led the chase to catch the errant skater before he crossed the state line and was out of Maurice's jurisdiction. Adams thought that he was catching up to his quarry when his feet went out from under him and Lathrop and the minister fell on him. Maurice tried to hurdle the pile of skaters, but fell and broke a rib as the other pursuers all took nasty spills on the ice. It became clear to them that

Silliman had dropped all of the sand in his pockets on the ice to delay his pursuers.

The bruised skaters returned to the fire where they heard that the neighing horse had been stolen by Silliman and was abandoned when he became lame. The men agreed that Silliman had devised an ingenious escape. Silliman exchanged Saunder's skates for a night's lodging in Owego and went to Rochester, where he swindled a crowd out of nine dollars that they had paid to observe him skating on all fours. Silliman traveled eastward along the canal until he reached Syracuse, where he had handbills printed to announce his skating demonstration.

The ice had become slushy by the time he reached Utica, where he stole a mare to ride to Oswego. He sold the mare there and boarded the sloop, *Fairaway,* to escape to Canada. The Oneida County Horse-Thief Society chased him to Lake Ontario but couldn't catch him. Captain Asa Birdmaster of the *Fairaway* asked no questions of his passengers. His only criteria was that a passenger's money was current and negotiable.

That concluded Grandfather Adams' story to his grandsons. They may not have been able to skate that day, but they had found another form of entertainment. Grandfather Adams admitted that Four-Skate Pilkington was the most rascally devil that he had met in his lifetime. Pilkington, or Silliman, never returned to New York State, and no one was sorry that he stayed away.

Repairing a Breach

The Finger Lakes Region experienced heavy rains during the fall of 1827. Tom Culver, the pathmaster for the section of the Erie Canal west of the Montezuma marshes, was patrolling the canal looking for leaks. The level in all of the streams feeding the canal was up, and therefore the water level of the canal was high. The pressure on the sides of the canal grew as the rain continued. While walking along the towpath late one evening in September, Culver noticed swirling water along the embankment across the canal.

Several hundred yards up the canal, Culver could see the bridge that joined the two parcels of Abel Stitt's farm that had been split by the construction of the canal. The pathmaster couldn't take the time to use the bridge; he waded across the four-foot-deep canal to check the embankment near the swirling water. He saw that the bank was riddled with holes made by muskrats. They had burrowed in the soft dirt of the embankment to make homes that they had recently abandoned.

Culver began to pack the holes with stones and straw, but there were too many of them for his patching to be effective. He heard a sucking sound as a large chunk of the bank fell into the canal. He realized that this was not a one-man repair job. Culver hurried toward Lyons. On the edge of town, he saw the lights of Ephraim Rowbottom's tavern, the Pride of the West. The pathmaster entered the tavern and asked Rowbottom how many guests he had that night. Rowbottom replied that there were sixteen men and five ladies.

Culver called upstairs, "The Erie's breaching at Stitt's Crossing. All good men and true, up and out." Thirteen of the men agreed to help; the other three were too old to do strenuous work. Culver walked into the taproom to ask for help. The sippers at the bar asked what was in it for them if they helped. They were told that they would earn twelve and a half cents an hour for work with an ax, pick, or shovel. When they responded that they had no tools, Rowbottom said that he would supply them. Culver got four volunteers from the bar; he did not have as much confidence in them as he had in the other thirteen men from the Pride of the West.

Culver then went looking for Lyons' chief constable, whom he found playing poker at the Eagle House. Within ten minutes Lyons' churchbells were pealing, rifles were fired into the air, horns were blowing, and the 1812 carronade on the green had been fired to alert people of the breach. The cry in the streets was, "Erie's draining out at Stitt's Crossing! All out to staunch the break!" Culver was told at the Eagle House that the hurry-up boat was moored at Harris' Basin, two miles west of Lyons.

The "hurry-up" boat was a thirty-foot maintenance and repair boat commanded by a section superintendent and manned by former canal builders. It was equipped with material such as chains, girders, joists, mattocks, mauls, picks, planks, ropes, spades, and other maintenance and repair gear. It was called the hurry-up boat because it was pulled by three of the fastest horses on the canal and traveled at ten to twelve miles an hour. Passenger boats on the canal moved along at four miles a hour, and cargo boats were even slower.

Culver borrowed a horse and rode to Harris' Basin, where he pounded on the door of the hurry-up boat and called out, "Breached!" Superintendent Glenn answered the door, admitted that he had been expecting trouble, and asked about the location of the breach. Culver told Glenn that his men were needed at Stitt's Crossing. Glenn called out to them to be ready with their kits in three minutes.

Culver rode on looking for volunteers from farms along the route back to the breach. He stopped at the first farmhouse and was greeted by a farmer pointing a loaded musket at him. Culver told him of the breach and offered to pay him twelve and a half cents an hour if he would help. The farmer signed on, and Culver asked him if he had any oxen or horses that could pull timber. Culver contracted for the farmer's yoke of oxen for seventy-five cents for the night. Culver asked him if he had any sons. He replied that he didn't, but that he had a wife who wasn't afraid of hard work. Culver signed her on for fifty cents for the night's work.

Culver stopped at several more farms looking for helpers on the way back to Stitt's Crossing. Most of the farmers came along to help, but a few turned him away. The pathmaster figured that he would have about 100 workers, including the people from Lyons, to help the hurry-up crew when he got back to the breach.

As he approached Stitt's Crossing, Culver was greeted by 150 people milling about in confusion. More people were arriving every moment, on foot, on horses or mules, and in homemade flat boats. The pathmaster asked where the hurry-up boat was. He was told that it was mudlarked (stuck in the mud) at the bottom of the canal about two miles away.

Many men were hauling dirt in wheelbarrows to the breach; as soon as they poured out their load of dirt, it washed back into the cornfields. Others were working with mauls and sledgehammers driving piles into the edge of the canal to hold a retaining wall. As soon as they finished pounding, the piles washed away. Culver heard a giant sucking sound as a large section of berm gave way, taking several volunteers with it. They struggled to safety.

Young women were working shoulder to shoulder with the men. Pioneer wives were used to hard labor. The older women were preparing pots of hot coffee and kettles of steaming soup. Young girls and boys were gathering brush and small limbs to keep the fires going.

Culver remembered the saying: "For a big breach, use big timber." He asked all of the lumbermen and sawyers to report to him. He directed them to farmer Stitt's timber lot, one-eighth mile to the east, and told them to cut and trim two- and three-foot diameter softwoods and to float them on the canal to the breach. The men wrapped chains around the felled trees and teams of oxen hauled them to the canal.

As Culver was standing near the breach waiting for the first timber to arrive, he heard the horn of the hurry-up boat arriving. It was one of the sweetest sounds that he had ever heard; he could now turn over the direction of the breach repair to the superintendent. Superintendent Glenn observed that the breach was large, and that many more large timbers were needed. The pathmaster was assured that more logs were on the way. As he was told this, they could see more elm and sycamore trunks floating to the site of the breach.

As they watched the additional timber arrive, the superintendent was told of another weak spot in the berm a quarter of a mile to the east. He ordered one of his senior men to take twenty workers and the necessary mauls, planks, posts, ropes, and wooden plugs to repair it. He told them to put mustard in their shoes and to get there before the bank of the canal gave way.

As the timber arrived at the opening in the canal, the superintendent's men used their peaveys to guide the logs into place at the breach. Then they used mauls and sledgehamers to drive in deep piles in the canal bank. About an hour after the superintendent's arrival, the big breach was repaired. As the sun was coming up, he told the workers to line up at the hurry-up boat to collect their pay.

Three workers were disabled with broken arms, legs, and ribs. A horse was lost in quicksand. The towpath had been ripped up and the punctured berm needed additional repair. Farmer Stitt had lost a section of his wood lot and about ten acres of corn that had been flooded.

Traffic resumed on the canal at noon on the following day. Such a breach in the canal bank was not a rarity. Breaks occurred about fifty times a season along the 364-mile length of the canal.

THE STUMP PULLER

One of the ingenious devices that helped the workers dig the Erie Canal was a giant stump puller. Two sixteen-foot diameter wheels were attached to the ends of twenty-inch diameter axle that was thirty feet long. In the middle of the axle was a third wheel fourteen feet in diameter with a rim that was broad enough to hold a rope or chain. A chain fixed around the stump was attached to the axle shaft, and chocks were placed under the two outer wheels.

When the horses or oxen pulled on a rope or chain that had been wound around the smaller wheel at the center of the shaft, the stump came out of the ground with ease—accompanied by the sound of the popping and snapping of roots.

The down-gear advantage of the fourteen-foot wheel over the axle shaft's twenty-inch diameter provided the considerable mechanical advantage that gave the stump puller its power. Seven men and two horses could pull forty stumps a day using this device. It was another example of the "Yankee ingenuity" that made the the canal possible.

Stump Puller

TYRONE POWER'S TRIP ON THE ERIE CANAL

Within ten years of the completion of the Erie Canal in 1825, many celebrities from Europe visited the United States to travel on the country's latest engineering marvel. During the 1830s, these visitors included royalty such as Duke Bernhard of Saxe-Weimar; Fanny Kemble, the actress; Captain Frederick Marryat, British naval officer and author; and Fanny Trollope, author and mother of the well-known British novelist, Anthony Trollope.

One of the travelers on the canal in the early 1830s was the Shakespearean actor, Tyrone Power. His descendant and namesake, movie actor Tyrone Power, starred in many adventure motion pictures, such as the swashbucklers, "Blood and Sand" and "The Mark of Zorro." The earlier Tyrone Power was touring the United States with an acting company and decided to experience travel on America's internationally acclaimed waterway.

Power was impressed with the engineering accomplishments of the canal but not with canalboat travel. Like most travelers, he found the canalboats uncomfortable and the travel slow and tedious. The small hammocks in the sleeping saloon were much too small for his frame. He couldn't sleep one evening on an eastbound canalboat out of Rochester, so he went on deck. The actor decided to remain on deck all night, but he hadn't counted on the hordes of mosquitoes that confronted him. He spent the night chain-smoking cigars to help to ward off the mosquitoes and slapping those that got through his smoke screen.

One of the natives of the area admitted to Power that the mosquitoes were particularly pesky that night. He told the actor, "Them's the real galinippers. Come all the way north for the summer from the Red River. Let a man go to sleep with them chaps around and if he puts his head in a cast iron kettle, they'd make a sieve of it by morning. Why, they're strong enough to lift a canal boat out of the water, if only they could get their bills underneath her!"

Workers from Ireland

In 1817, the digging of the Erie Canal began near Rome. The progress made during the first spring, summer, and fall was disappointing. The Canal Commision warned the contractors that unless better progress was made in 1818, there would be no more contracts—maybe there would be no canal. Rome and Oneida Counties had learned that they couldn't dig the canal alone. Even with the help of men from neighboring counties, there weren't enough laborers to meet the construction schedule. Farms, mills, and stores required men to staff them. Laborers on the canal were required from sunrise until sunset, six days a week. Building a canal was not a part-time job.

Some work could be done during the winter, including removing underbrush along the route and building bunk houses and tool sheds for the laborers. Contractors paid 50¢ for the use of a horse for two days. Wages varied widely: axeman, $1.00 a day; boy, 30¢ a day; carpenter, $1.00 a day; and grubber (brush remover), 47¢ a day.

Ireland was an important source of labor at that time. In 1818, Ireland was a hungry country; over 1,700 Irish immigrants passed through Ellis Island in New York that year. Those that emigrated from Ireland were not of the poorest class; the poor could not afford passage. However, many of those who did immigrate to the United States were penniless upon their arrival in their new country. They were met by canal contractors; jobs were readily available. They were told that wages were 50¢ a day and "found" (board and lodging). Contractors were impressed with their work. The Irish proved to be better diggers than the farmers, mill hands, and shopkeepers who had done the digging in the first season. Many of them were experienced diggers from the peat bogs of Ireland.

Workers could choose to be paid by the hour or "by the job," that is, by the amount of earth they could remove. Three-man teams were established; rivalry among the teams was fierce. The most ambitious teams voted to be paid by the job at twelve and a half cents per cubic yard of earth removed. In five and a half days, a good team could dig fifty feet of canal including building a towpath on one side and a berm on the other. Since the canal was forty feet wide at the top, twenty-eight feet wide at the bottom, and four feet deep, this meant removing 250 cubic yards of dirt. Each member of the team earned $1.88 per day, a very respectable wage in 1818.

One myth about the canal is that it was built by the Irish. Immigration to the United States from Ireland did not reach significant numbers until the 1830s. Until that time, most of the foreign laborers were English and German. The wages of more than $1.00 a day on the canal were three times what workers could earn at home. Although no one questions the considerable contribution that laborers from Ireland made to the construction of the "big ditch," historians estimate that one-quarter of the workforce was Irish.

In addition to their hard work, the Irish were known for their Saturday night fights. A popular ballad of the day was about that aspect of their life:

Paddy on the Canal

I learned for to be very handy;
To use both the shovel and spade;
I learned the whole art of canalling;
I think it an excellent trade.

I learned for to be very handy,
Although I was not very tall,
I could handle the "sprig of Shillelah,"
With the best man on the canal.

Erie Canal at Adams Basin

• chapter three •

Villages Along the Canal – West to East

He saw, as widely spreads the unchannell'd plain
Where inland realms for ages bloom'd in vain,
Canals, long winding, ope a watery flight,
And distant streams, and seas and lakes unite.
From fair Albany, toward the falling sun,
Back through the midland lengthening channels run;
Meet the far lake, the beauteous towns that lave,
And Hudson joined to broad Ohio's wave.

From *Vision of Columbus* by Joel Barlow

THE ERIE CANAL TRAVERSES THE FINGER LAKES REGION'S NORTHERNMOST FOUR COUNTIES—MONROE, WAYNE, CAYUGA, AND ONONDAGA. SINCE THE ERIE CANAL HAS GONE THROUGH THREE DIFFERENT CONFIGURATIONS, A FEW VILLAGES THAT USED TO BE ON THE CANAL, SUCH AS PORT BYRON, WEEDSPORT, AND JORDAN, ARE NO LONGER ALONG ITS ROUTE. WHEN THE CANAL WAS REROUTED TO THE NORTH TO TAKE ADVANTAGE OF ONEIDA LAKE IN ITS THIRD CONFIGURATION, SYRACUSE WAS NO LONGER ON THE CANAL. THE OLD ERIE CANAL STATE PARK, A LINEAR PARK BETWEEN SYRACUSE AND ROME, MARKS AN EARLIER, ABANDONED ROUTE OF THE CANAL.

A BRIEF DESCRIPTION AND HISTORY ARE PROVIDED HERE FOR THE VILLAGES ALONG THE CANAL'S CURRENT ROUTE.

BROCKPORT

Brief History

In 1817, Hiel Brockway, a Connecticut-born Ontario County builder, moved to the town of Sweden with his wife, Phoebe, and their twelve children. He purchased large parcels of land on the west side of Lake Road. In 1821, James Seymour, a Clarkson merchant, bought land on the east side of Lake Road. Some of Seymour's purchases were in partnership with Abel Baldwin and Myron Holley, who was a member of the Canal Commission. During the 1820s, Brockway owned or had a part-interest in most of the land that became Brockport, including Seymour's land on the east side of Lake Road.

Lots were surveyed, and streets were laid out to avoid the poorly-drained, swampy area in what is now downtown. In 1822, construction of homes and commercial buildings began on both sides of Main Street from just north of the Erie Canal to north of

College Street. Most of the homes and stores were constructed of brick, which was produced locally at a cost of $3.00 a thousand. The Native Americans called Brockport "The Red Village" because of the red brick used in its construction.

On November 15, 1822, at "a numerous and respectable meeting of the inhabitants of the towns of Sweden and Clarkson," the name "Brockport"—a shortened version of "Brockway's Port"—was formally adopted. The meeting was presided over by Hiel Brockway at Brick Tavern, Sylvester Alvord's hotel at Clarkson Corners. On November 19, 1822, the Rochester *Telegraph* noted the event in an article: "NEW VILLAGE—A village, called Brockport, is now erecting on the place where the Grand Canal intersects the main road leading from Clarkson to LeRoy."

The Erie Canal was extended to Brockport in October 1823. A salute was fired to celebrate the first boat from the east, a scow, and the residents of the village turned out to cheer it along. In June 1825, Brockport residents cheered General LaFayette when he passed through on the canal and in October celebrated the procession of boats that formally opened the canal. While Brockport was the western terminus of the canal, it "created a large amount of business here, and under its impetus the village thrived." In 1835, 451,000 bushels of grain were transported through Brockport on the way to the mills of Rochester, the "Flour City."

In addition to Brockway and Seymour, among the early settlers of Brockport were George Allen, John G. Davis, Joshua Field, Thomas Roby, and Luke Webster. Some of the settlers were from Connecticut and New Hamphire, but most were from elsewhere in New York. In 1830, the population of the village was 685.

Hiel Brockway set aside a six-acre "college lot" at the end of College Street. In 1834, the Brockport Collegiate Institute was opened under the auspices of the Baptist Missionary Conference. The Insititute evolved into the State University of New York—College at Brockport.

In 1831, Cyrus McCormick, a blacksmith from West Virginia, invented a reaper for harvesting wheat. It could harvest as much wheat as seven men harvesting by hand. McCormick spent a number of years in Washington, D.C., obtaining a patent for his invention and improving its design. While in Washington, he met Brockport Congressman E. B. Holmes. McCormick had been looking for someone to manufacture his reapers, and Holmes told him about Brockport's Bacchus and Burroughs foundry that had been manufacturing farm implements since 1828.

In 1844, McCormick moved to Brockport and contracted Bacchus and Burroughs to make 100 harvesters to his design. The inventor encountered problems with the first 100 reapers that were built. However, on Frederick Root's farm in the town of Sweden, one of them became the first machine to harvest wheat in the United States. In 1846, McCormick ordered another 100 harvesters to be built at the small canal-side shop of Dayton S. Morgan and William H. Seymour. McCormick was much more satisfied with the second 100 machines. One of these machines is on display in Henry Ford's museum at Greenfield Village in Michigan.

Although the Genesee region had been the wheat basket of the country in the late 1700s and early 1800s, the center of wheat production moved to the Midwest in the late 1800s. McCormick moved to Chicago and became wealthy manufacturing harvesters. Brockport continued to be a center for the manufacture of farm equipment into the 1890s, when the shift of wheat production to the Midwest was accompanied by the relocation of the manufacturing of farm equipment there.

Frederick Root, on whose farm the first grain had been harvested by machinery, invented a grain cleaner and separator. In 1851, William H. Seymour manufactured the automatic raking reaper, which he called "the quadrant platform." Seymour's old partner, Dayton S. Morgan, manufactured his line of Triumph reapers for twenty years until 1894, when his factory was destroyed by fire.

The Bacchus and Burroughs foundry was taken over by the Johnson Harvester factory, which employed just under 500 people and turned out 6,000 machines during its peak year in 1882. That year the Bacchus and Burroughs factory burned down and manufacturing was moved to Batavia.

Mary Jane Holmes and her husband, Daniel, lived in a cottage on College Street, where Mary Jane wrote thirty-eight romantic novels over a fifty-one-year period. Her first novel, *Tempest and Sunshine*, a tale of Southern society based on her experiences when she lived in Kentucky, was published in 1854 and was an immediate success. She wrote from one to three books a year from 1854 through 1905 and earned an average of $6,000 for her novels, a substantial amount of money in the last half of the nineteenth century.

Mary Jane also wrote stories for magazines, such as the New York *Weekly*, and many of her novels were serialized in New York periodicals. Although she lived in Brockport from 1853 until her death in 1907, the scenes of most of her novels were in New England, the South, and Europe.

Another economic activity in the history of the Brockport area was bean farming. In the 1880s, more beans were shipped from Brockport than any other location in the United States. The village became known as the bean center of America. Eventually, as with wheat, the production of beans moved westward.

THE CANAL

Brockport has two liftbridges over the Erie Canal, with a transient mooring between them on the south bank. A small picnic area is located there, and a plaque in Harvester Park near the Park Avenue liftbridge commemorates the invention of the reaper by Cyrus McCormick.

The Seymour Library, located at 49 State Street, also houses the Brockport museum, which has multiple floors of collections that depict the history of Brockport. The Liftbridge Bookstore on Main Street has an excellent selection of reading material.

ADAMS BASIN

BRIEF HISTORY

In 1827, the brothers Marcus and Myron Adams moved from Bloomfield to Adams Basin, which was called Kings-Adams Basin. It was named for the company formed by Bradford and Moses King and Abner Adams, the father of Marcus and Myron. That year, the hamlet had a boat yard, a dry dock, a pail factory, and a sawmill with a lath machine and a shingle machine. Marcus Adams opened a store on the canal, built horse barns and a storehouse, erected a lumber mill on Salmon Creek, and planted apple and peach orchards on a 97-acre farm. He was the first postmaster of Adams Basin, which was named for William Adams, a relative of Marcus and Myron.

Alexander Milliner, General George Washington's drummer boy, was born in Adams Basin. A New York State historic marker is located in front of the Milliner family home on Canal Road, just west of the hamlet. Milliner is buried in Mt. Hope Cemetery in Rochester.

Adams Basin became known by workers on the Erie Canal as the place where local farmers sold broken-down horses to canal drivers at inflated prices. Local historian Bud Nichols noted, "Adams wrote that from Albany to Buffalo, Adams Basin was known for its worthless gang of harpies, who would take advantages of the canalers."

On July 1, 1852, the Rochester, Lockport and Niagara Railroad opened a station in Adams Basin. Marcus Adams was the first station agent. In the late 1850s, the Adams family moved to Niagara Falls.

THE CANAL

The hamlet of Adams Basin is located between Brockport and Spencerport where Washington Street, Route 36, crosses the Erie Canal on the Adams Basin Bridge. The Salmon Creek Golf Club and Twin Hills Golf Course are located north of the canal on the west side of Washington Street.

The Canalside Inn, a bed and breakfast inn known locally as the Adams-Ryan House, is on the National Register of Historic Places. The Inn provides docking services. The post-and-beam house was built in the early 1800s and became the first general store in the community in 1827. From 1890 until 1915, it was a tavern called the Ryan House.

Northampton Park is located south of Route 31 (Spencerport Road) and west of Route 36 near Adams Basin. Access is from Colby Street, Hubbell Road, Route 36, Salmon Creek and Route 31, and Sweden-Walker Road. The 973-acre park has trails for hiking and horseback riding. Northampton Park also has two lodges, a playground, two softball fields, and facilities for group camping (which requires a special permit). In the winter, the park is an active ski center with a rope-tow ski area, a ski school, sledding hills, cross-county ski trails, and a warming shelter.

Springdale Farm, an educational farm, is operated within Northampton Park. It has beef cattle, chickens, dairy cattle, dairy goats, ducks, pigs, sheep, and turkeys. The farm also has field crops, a fruit orchard, herb gardens, hiking trails, pastures, a pond, vegetable gardens, and a five-acre wood lot. Springdale Farm is open all year. Admission is free; group tours can be scheduled.

The expanse of water on the canal east of Adams Basin houses the New York State Department of Transportation Waterways maintenance craft, including dredgers, scows, and small tugboats called tenders. The Adams Basin Marina is located at 651 Gallup Road, Spencerport.

SPENCERPORT

BRIEF HISTORY

In August, 1802, George Warren Willey of East Haddam, Connecticut, became the first settler in Spencerport in the southern part of the town of Parma, which later became the town of Ogden. He had attended the "Genesee meeting" in East Haddam at which James Wadsworth told of hewing a fertile and prosperous countryside out of the wilderness. Willey signed up for land at $2.00 an acre. He came to the area on the old Indian trail from the village of Canawaugus to Braddocks Bay. The trail was called the Canawaugus Trail, then Canawaugus Road, and finally Union Street (Route 259).

The four Colby brothers, Abraham, Ephraim, Isaac, and Timothy, were the next setttlers to arrive in the village. The three Spencer brothers, Austin, Daniel, and William H., were also early residents, as were members of the Hill, Nichols, True, and Webster families. Daniel Spencer purchased most of the land in what had become the village of Spencerport. It was known as Spencer's Basin when the first Post Office was established. Daniel operated a grist mill, a lumber yard, and a saw mill and manufactured linseed oil.

The Erie Canal through Spencerport opened in 1823. In the early 1900s, the Rochester, Lockport and Buffalo Railroad was built through Spencerport. Early industries in the village were a cannery, a blast furnace, and a tannery. Spencerport was also known for the manufacture of fireworks and farm implements, including the Hoy potato digger. In 1890, the village was a principal shipping center for cabbage grown in the region.

The Canal

Union Street crosses the canal on a liftbridge, near which there is transient mooring. Captain Jeff's Marina is at 416 Elmgrove Road. Spencerport Canal Park is located east of the liftbridge on the south bank of the canal. In 1973, The original control tower for the liftbridge was relocated to Pulver House Museum at 696 Colby Street, off Union Street on the grounds of Springdale Farm.

Guard gate 11 is located a mile east of Spencerport, near the Gillette Road Bridge. Located another three and a half miles to the east on the north bank of the canal is a cove where the present Erie Canal swings south to pass to the south of Rochester. The "old" Erie Canal continued eastward to the downtown Rochester where it crossed the Genesee River on a stone aqueduct. The "old" Erie Canal has been filled in and is now Broad Street and the Route 490 Expressway.

ROCHESTER (south of)

THE CANAL

Over thirty bridges span the ten miles of the Erie Canal that circumvents Rochester to the south. The most aesthetic are the gray stone "parabolic" (shallow-arc) bridges designed by Frederic Law Olmstead, who plannned Central Park in New York City. One is located on the west side of the Genesee River, and two are on east side linking Genesee Valley Park to Rochester. Red Creek enters the canal between these two east-side bridges. Just east of the Genesee River, a cut of sixty-three feet was required to reroute the canal. To the east of that section, an embankment forty-two feet high had to be constructed as the canal traversed a low-lying area.

The Henrietta lock, Lock 33, is located four miles east of the Genesee River. West from Lock 33 is a lock-free section of the canal appoximately sixty-five miles long. Clover Street lock, Lock 32, is located 1.3 miles east of Lock 33. During the days when the canal had heavy commercial traffic, a large surge pool was constructed on the north side of the canal just west of Lock 32 to prevent water dumped from Lock 33 from flooding the surrounding land. Sunken hulks of boats in the surge pool are the only reminders of its earlier connection with the canal.

North of Lock 32, New York State maintains a canal park with picnic benches and cook-out facilities. This site has an observation deck above the lock on the north side of the canal that is ideal for taking pictures of boats being locked through. The best mooring is west of the lock; there is a turbulent outflow east of the lock. The aeration of the water east of the lock attracts many fishermen.

PITTSFORD

BRIEF HISTORY

In 1789, the brothers Israel and Simon Stone, who were Revolutionary War veterans, built the first house near a big spring just west of the State Street bridge in Pittsford, which was known over the years as Northfield, Boyle, and Smallwood. Following the Stones were other veterans of the Revolution, including Captain Henry Gale who was sentenced to hang for his part in Shay's Rebellion in Massachusetts but was later pardoned.

In 1792, the first physician, Dr. John Ray, arrived in the village, and two years later the first schoolhouse was built. In 1803, a library was built at the foot of Tobey Hill, and one year later Simon Stone, the village's first lawyer, established an office. In 1807, the Phoenix Hotel was built at the four corners of the village. Famous visitors who stayed there included Governor DeWitt Clinton, General LaFayette, and Daniel Webster. In 1812, the Hargous House was built at 52 South Main Street. It was a station on the Underground Railroad in the days leading up to the Civil War.

The original Erie Canal that was dedicated in 1825 followed the course of South Street in the village. The present Erie Canal passes through the village to the east of the earlier canal.

THE CANAL

The canal passes under Monroe Avenue (Route 31) and Main Street as it wends its way through the village of Pittsford. It passes by Schoen Place, a street of upscale shops along the canal.

Along the canal at Schoen Place, boats can tie up at an esplanade. Across the canal, on its south side, are additional bollards for tying up and a small picnic area. An old grain mill operates along the canal. It feeds the ducks and geese on the waterway, which stay there year-round. Frequently, traffic in the road along the canal stops until the ducks and geese complete their crossing.

BUSHNELLS BASIN

THE CANAL

East of the village of Pittsford, beautiful homes line the canal on both sides. For the next five miles, the canal follows a V-shaped course crossing the Irondequoit Valley, where the embankment is eighty feet high, as it moves eastward to Bushnells Basin. Where the canal crosses Irondequoit Creek, manhole covers provide access to the the creek eighty feet below, allowing the embankment to be checked periodically. A guard gate is positioned at each end of the embankment in case of water loss through the banks of the canal. Marsh Road bridge is one half mile east of guard gate 10. Richardson's Canal House Inn and Loud's Tavern are on the south bank of the canal.

Richardson's Canal House, located at 1474 Marsh Road in Pittsford, is the oldest Erie Canal tavern surviving in its original form that is still on canal water. The tavern was built in 1818, restored in 1979, and is now listed in the National Register of Historic Places. Museum-quality antiques and artifacts help to capture the atmosphere and style of the tavern in its early days.

The restaurant features a seasonal menu inspired by French country and American regional cooking. Dinners are served in the restaurant dining rooms; informal suppers are served in the Cobblestone Pub or the Canalside Terrace (in season).

Oliver Loud's Inn, adjacent to the Canal House Tavern, is an historic country inn built in 1812. It has museum-quality paintings, china, and furnishings. Guest rooms, such as the Garland Room, have luxurious appointments that recall the private quarters of a country manor.

FAIRPORT

BRIEF HISTORY

In 1789, Glover Perrin, for whom the town of Perinton is named, built a home on Ayrault Road and became the area's first settler. Between 1796 and 1802, he held, at various times, most of the important offices in the town: assessor, constable, highway commissioner, and school commissioner. John and Martin Sperbeck were other early settlers. Most of the early settlers were from New England.

On May 26, 1812, the town of Perinton was established from the portions of the townships of Northfield and Boyle. Before the Erie Canal was built, Fairport consisted of a block house, a frame house, and seven log houses. In 1822, the packet boat, *Myron Holley,* tied up at Fairport and put the village on the map. In 1827, Prichard Tavern, later known as the Fairport Hotel, was built on Main street.

In 1852, Daniel B. DeLand, a former canal boat captain, established a baking soda plant on the bank of the canal. It became Fairport's principal industry. Henry A. DeLand and Levi J. DeLand succeeded Daniel DeLand in the business. Subsequently, Henry moved south and founded DeLand, Florida, and helped to establish Stetson University there. In 1893, the soda factory suffered a disastrous fire. The business declined but continued until 1928.

In 1853, the railroad, which eventually became part of the New York Central, came to Fairport. The village of Fairport was incorporated in 1867. The production of cans began in Fairport in 1881 when the Cobb family established the Sanitary Can Company, which pioneered in the manufacture of solderless, double-seamed cans. Sanitary Can was sold to the American Can Company in 1908. Later Fairport products were vinegar and pectin, which is used in canning.

The Canal

The village of Fairport has taken farsighted steps to promote the use of the canal. Fairport Village Landing Mall is on the south bank of the canal along the west side of Main Street. The Fairport Historical Museum at 18 Perrin Street is located behind the mall. The Packett's Landing complex is on the east side of Main Street. An old box factory has been tastefully restored with shops and a restaurant across the canal from Packett's Landing.

The liftbridge that carries Main Street over the canal is unique in that it slopes downward from south to north and is raised and lowered at an angle. Transient boat moorings are located between the Main Street liftbridge and the Parker Street bridge. Perinton Park, located just west of the village along the north bank of the canal, has a small floating dock and a picnic area.

MACEDON

Brief History

In the spring of 1789, Webb Harwood and his wife, the first settlers of Macedon, moved to the area from Adams, Massachusetts. The Harwoods, who were accompanied by Bennett Bates, Noah Porter, and Jonathan Warner, built their log home a half mile east of the village, near the first canal lock west of Palmyra. Abraham Lapham built the first frame house just before 1800. The first schoolhouse was built about the same time north of the present canal, a half mile from the west lock in Macedon. In 1805, Walter Walker built the first blacksmith shop. The first inn was built on William Porter's farm about 1810. In 1817, Thomas Hance from Maryland built the first store in Macedon. Until 1825, most of the trade at his frame store was conducted by barter.

The first town meeting for the six-mile-square town of Macedon was held on February 11, 1823. The village of Macedon was incorporated in November 1856 on a one-mile-square site.

Routes 31 and 31F are the main east-west routes through the town; Route 350 is the principal north-south route. Macedon's largest industry after World War II was Kordite, founded by Richard and Howard Samuels. It subsequently became the Plastics Division of Mobil Chemical and the Packaging Division of Tenneco.

The Canal

West of Macedon, the canal parallels the old New York Central Railroad. The canal widens in three places in this section, because the present canal was routed alongside the earlier canal that it replaced. Just west of the Wayneport bridge, the Fairport Yacht Club moors its boats in the old Erie Canal. East of the Canandaigua Road bridge, the old and new canals are separated by small islands. The 1862 canal route, south of the present canal, was closer to the village of Macedon. Lock 30 in Macedon is near the end of Railroad Avenue. The site of Lock 61 on the 1862 Erie Canal is just east of Route 350.

PALMYRA

Brief History

Palmyra, named for the Syrian city, is located at the intersection of Routes 21 and 31. The first settlers were surveyors John Jenkins and John Swift who came from the Wyoming Valley of Pennsylvania in 1789. Swift built a log house on Ganargua Creek, at the eastern boundary of the present village of Palmyra. In the Iroquois language, "Ganargua" means "a village, suddenly sprung up." Swift built mills at Canal and Main Streets; he became the first citizen of the village, which was known as Swift's Landing. Swift trained militia during the War of 1812 and attained the rank of general. He was killed at the Battle of Queenstown Heights.

In 1791, a group of families from Rhode Island settled in Palmyra. They included the Durfee family, who planted the first apple orchards in the area. David Wilcox, Winston Churchill's great-grandfather, was one of the settlers from Rhode Island. Louis Philippe, later the "Citizen King" of France, stayed with the Durfees on a tour of the region in 1796. Swift's Landing was renamed Palmyra in 1797.

Joseph Smith, Sr., moved to Palmyra in 1816 from Royalton, Vermont, with his wife, three daughters, and six sons. Joseph, Jr., was the third-oldest son. The family moved to a farm about four miles south of Palmyra in 1818, where Joseph, Jr., was visited by the angel Moroni and founded the Mormon religion in 1827. The Book of Mormon was printed in the Grandin Building in Palmyra in 1830.

The completion of the Erie Canal in 1825 brought an economic boom to the village. The boatyard at Palmyra built the packet boats *Myron Holley* and the *Twin Brothers*, owned by John and Levi Thayer. Henry Wells of Wells-Fargo is a favorite son of Palmyra. He began his career by delivering packages around the village on foot and then by horse and wagon. He founded the Wells and Company express agency; later, he teamed up with Henry Fargo to run the pony express in the western United States.

The Alling Coverlet Museum is located at 122 William Street in Palmyra, and the "corner of four churches" is located at the intersection of Routes 21 and 31 in the village. A church occupies each of the four corners of the intersection. The First United Methodist Church, the Western Presbyterian Church, the Zion Episcopal Church, and the First Baptist Church are each on a corner. The Palmyra Macedon Aqueduct County Park is located at Erie Canal Lock 29, which is at the western edge of Palmyra on Route 31 in the town of Macedon. Swift's Landing County Park is located on Hogsback Road, off Route 223 in the town of Palmyra.

The Canal

The old canal and the new canal are parallel to each another; the old canal is closer to the village. The ruins of the aqueduct that used to carry the Erie Canal over Ganargua Creek are located at Lock 29, the site of Aqueduct Park. Biking and hiking trails link up with the towpath on the south side of the canal between Lock 29 and the Division Street bridge. East of the village, a spillway made from an 1840s aqueduct channels excess water to Ganargua Creek, which is just north of the canal at this point. Swift's Landing County Park is just east of the spillway. East of the park, the canal passes though a narrow cutting, rounds Galloway Hill, turns southward for two miles, and then widens again near the village of Port Gibson.

The canal loops southward to the village of Port Gibson, the only Ontario County site on the canal. When the canal was being planned, its route was modified to ensure that Ontario County, a large prosperous county, would have a shipping point on the canal. Widewater County Park is located at the eastern end of the widewater. The park has picnic facilities and a launch ramp for small boats.

NEWARK

BRIEF HISTORY

The village of Newark is located in the town of Arcadia at the intersections of Routes 31 and 88. The first settlers of Newark cleared land along Ganargua Creek in 1791. Three Lusk brothers bought a one-square-mile tract that included the present site of Newark in 1806; however, the real development of the village began with the construction of the Erie Canal. The father of Newark is considered to be Joseph Miller; he bought 100 acres in 1819 from the Lusks, laid out streets, and sold lots. Miller had the contract for building one and a quarter miles of the Erie Canal through the area.

The hamlets of Lockville and Miller's Basin were consolidated in 1823 into the village of Newark, which was named for Newark, New Jersey. Some Newark natives claim that the village was named for the English Viscount Newark, who was co-proprietor of the site under the royal grant of the King of England.

For a century beginning in 1873, Newark was one of the rose capitals of the United States. C. H. Stuart and his father-in-law,

Albert Jackson, founded the Jackson-Perkins nurseries of the C. H. Stuart Company that year. At its peak, the nurseries had 400 employees planting, cultivating, packing, and shipping 12,000 plants per year, which included 400 varieties and a multitude of colors. The Jackson-Perkins two-acre experimental garden was visited by thousands of people. The nurseries were closed in the 1970s, when the company was consolidated with another nursery on the west coast.

The Newark Canal County Park is at the intersection of Route 88 and Van Buren Street; Erie Canal Lock 28B is in the village. Widewaters County Park is west of Newark on Route 31 in the town of Arcadia. The Hoffman Clock Museum, a gem of a museum housed in the Newark Public Library, has over 100 timepieces on display—mainly nineteenth-century American clocks. The Wayne County Extension Center of Finger Lakes Community College is located in the Maple Building of the Newark Developmental Center.

The Canal

Lock 28B is in downtown Newark, near the railroad bridge over the canal. Adjacent to the lock is the powerhouse that used to supply the power for its operation. Lock 59 from the 1862 Erie Canal, a double lock that allowed two-way traffic, is located just east of Lock 28B. The canal passes through marshes for three and a half miles east of Newark between hills with a 600-foot elevation. The old canal can be seen from the new canal in this section.

LYONS

BRIEF HISTORY

Lyons, the county seat of Wayne County, is located at the intersection of Routes 14 and 31. Charles Williamson, land agent for a group of English land speculators headed by Lord Pulteney, explored the area around Lyons in 1794. Williamson named the site of the joining of Ganargua Creek and the Canandaigua Lake outlet Lyons, because it reminded him of a smaller version of the confluence of the Saone and Rhone Rivers at Lyons, France. In 1789, Nicholas and William Stansell and their brother-in-law, John Featherly, became the first settlers in the area. They built a log cabin where the Canandaigua Lake outlet flows into Ganargua Creek to form the Clyde River.

In 1830, area farmers began to grow mint, and, by 1868, there were 300 acres of mint under cultivation. H. G. Hotchkiss began his peppermint and essential oils business on Water Street in 1841; by 1877, his facilities in Lyons were the largest in the world. He shipped his product worldwide, but most of his exports went to England. Hotchkiss became known as the "peppermint king." He was awarded prizes for his products in America, and his peppermint extracts won medals in expositions in London, Paris, and Vienna. Peppermint cultivation shifted to the Midwest, principally to Indiana and Michigan, but the leaves were still shipped to Lyons to be processed and bottled in the familiar amber bottles.

Included among Lyons' favorite sons are Admiral Willard Bronson, who was Commandant of the U.S. Naval Academy; Admiral Bradley Fiske, who fought with Admiral Dewey at the Battle of Manila Bay during the Spanish-American War; and William Stewart, U.S. Senator from Nevada and promoter of the Comstock Lode.

Erie Canal Lock 27 and the Barge Canal Dry Dock Marina are located in the village. Lyons is also the home of Abbey Park on Water Street and the hiking trails of the Blue Cut County Nature Center, which is located west of the village on Route 31. Lock Berlin County Park is located east of Lyons at Newark and Gansz Roads in the town of Galen.

THE CANAL

Drydock Lock 28A is just west of the village. It is a New York State Department of Transportation waterway depot and usually contains maintenance vessels undergoing repair. The canal utilizes the bed of Ganargua Creek from the point of its entry to the canal to Lock 27 in the village. Canandaigua Creek enters the canal east of Lock 27; it joins with Ganargua Creek to form the Clyde River, which is used by the Erie Canal for the next three miles. The three configurations of the Erie Canal each took a separate route from Lyons to Clyde. The original canal looped to the north and back via Pilgrimport and Lock Berlin roads, the enlargement built between 1835 and 1862 took an eastwardly course, and the present canal turns south following the course of the Clyde River. The Clyde River and the canal separate three miles east of Lyons; the canal follows man-made channels while the river meanders.

CLYDE

BRIEF HISTORY

The village of Clyde is located at the intersection of Routes 31 and 414. Originally named Block House, it was founded as a fort to protect British fur trade routes. In 1815, Frederick DeZeng, the "Father of Clyde," settled at the site of the Block House, which was then named Lauraville for one of Lord Pulteney's daughters. It was renamed Clyde in 1818 by Andrew McNab, since it reminded the Scottish land agent of Scotland. A replica of the 1700s Block House was constructed in 1975; it contains local artifacts. The building of the Erie Canal contributed significantly to the development of the village. The canal flows through Clyde; Lock 26 is just southeast of the village.

DeZeng donated land to Clyde for a village park. DeZeng's great-grandson, DeLancey Stowe, authorized drilling a well in the park, which yielded mineral water instead of the fresh water he had expected. Townspeople initially hoped that the discovery of mineral springs would lead to the development of a spa, but they decided to forego the commercialism that would have resulted.

The Galen Historical Society museum is located on Sodus Street in Clyde. Housed in the old Ketchem and Maloy mill, it contains some of the mill's original equipment. Black Brook County Park in the town of Galen is east of Clyde on old Route 31.

THE CANAL

The Erie Canal and the Clyde River rejoin just west of Clyde. The remains of Lock 53 from the second configuration of the canal is just west of the village. Lock 26 on the present canal is two and a half miles east of the village. Lock 26 has a pivoted taintor gate used to control the water level. The gate is required because the canal uses the Clyde River in this section, and the water level is subject to fluctuation. The canal runs southeast from Clyde; the Clyde River flows in and out of the canal three times.

The canal passes through the 6,432-acre Montezuma Wildlife Refuge, and the canal and the Clyde River separate again one mile west of Lock 25 at Mays Point. The Cayuga-Seneca Canal joins the canal one and a half miles east of Lock 25 for three miles. The Cayuga-Seneca Canal, a 17-mile-long waterway with four locks, joins the Erie Canal with the two largest Finger Lakes, Seneca Lake and Cayuga Lake. To the north, the Erie Canal bypasses two Cayuga County villages, Port Byron and Weedsport, and the Onondaga County village of Jordan, all of which were on the original canal. North of Jordan, the Erie Canal passes through Cross Lake, which is five miles long and one mile wide, on its way eastward to Oneida Lake.

BALDWINSVILLE

BRIEF HISTORY

John McHarrie, a veteran of the Revolutionary War from Maryland, was the first settler on the site of the village of Baldwinsville. This pioneer of Scotch-Irish descent moved to the area in 1792. McHarrie built his cabin at the rapids, or rifts, on the Seneca River. He picked the location knowing that loaded boats using the Seneca River would need help getting through the rapids. Baldwinsville's first name was McHarrie's Rifts.

In 1797, Dr. Jonas C. Baldwin, who had been the physician for the Inland Lock Navigation Company at Little Falls, and his family traveled through the area on their way to Ovid, where they owned a military lot. They followed the usual east-west path up the Mohawk River and Wood Creek, across Oneida Lake, down the Oneida River, and up the Seneca River. Mrs. Baldwin was reluctant to leave Little Falls, so, to appease her, her husband told her that he would purchase the first site that struck her fancy. That site was on the north bank along the rifts of the Seneca River. Dr. Baldwin purchased the lot the following year.

In 1806, Dr. Baldwin used his influence to have a state road built between Onondaga Hill and the mouth of Ox Creek, continuing on to Oswego. The following year he built a grist mill near the mouth of Tannery Brook. It was later converted to a woolen mill by Kellogg & Farr.

In 1809, Dr. Baldwin purchased from the Inland Lock Navigation Company control of the water from the mouth of the Oneida River to Cayuga Lake. He constructed a canal and locks on the north side of the river. He was given the right for twenty years to collect a toll from all boats passing through his lock. Dr. Baldwin also established the first store in the hamlet, which he owned until 1814 when Otis Bigelow open the Bigelow store—a Baldwinsville landmark for fifty years.

In 1825, Dr. Baldwin's son, Stephen, purchased the land adjacent to the dam on the south side of the Seneca River and built a hydraulic canal to supply water power. Initially, two flour mills and a saw mill were built on the canal to take advantage of the hydropower. Between 1850 and 1895, a pump and steam engine plant, a hydroelectric plant, and a knitting mill were constructed on the north side of the river. On the south side, the saw mill was replaced by a distillery, which later was converted to a paper mill.

THE CANAL

Until the completion of the Erie Canal in 1825, Baldwinsville had always been a part of the east-west water transportation system. However, the Erie Canal bypassed Baldwinsville to the south, causing an economic downturn in the area. Later, the village was connected to the canal system via the junction of the Seneca River and the Oswego River at the Onondaga Lake outlet. In 1839, a towpath was constructed between Baldwinsville and Mud Lock, and, by 1850, two large locks had been constructed on the Oneida River for steamboat navigation. The State became responsible for the Baldwin rights to the dam and canal and built a larger lock in Baldwinsville in 1850.

In 1917, when the present route of the Erie Canal was completed, Baldwinsville again became part of the State's east-west water transportation system. The Erie Canal proceeds eastward from Baldwinsville on the Seneca River to the Oneida River and Oneida Lake from Three Rivers Point, the confluence of the Oneida, Oswego, and Seneca Rivers.

BREWERTON

BRIEF HISTORY

The Oneida Indians were the first inhabitants of the area around Brewerton. In 1759, the British built a fort at the western end of Oneida Lake, where the Oneida River flows out of the lake, to protect their interests from the French and their Indian allies. In 1766, the British abandoned the fort, which was later burned down by the Oneidas. Oliver Stevens was the first pioneer to settle in Brewerton after the Revolutionary War. He traded with the Oneidas and opened a tavern for the men who hauled cargo in bateaux on Oneida Lake and the Oneida River.

Brewerton was not on the Erie Canal when it opened in 1825. The original route of the canal was south of Oneida Lake through Syracuse. In 1832, a canal was built to link the Erie Canal with the eastern end of Oneida Lake, and the Oneida River, west of Brewerton, was dredged to aid navigation to the Seneca River. In 1849, two steamers were built in Brewerton to tow barges across Oneida Lake; however, they only operated for ten years until the Erie Canal was widened and deepened in the late 1850s. Today, Fort Brewerton on Route 11 is a place of interest in the area.

THE CANAL

Lock 23 between Black Creek Road and Caughdenoy Road near Brewerton is the busiest of the fifty-seven locks in the State's canal system. Transient mooring is provided below the lock on the south side. A canal park with picnic and cook-out areas is adjacent to the lock. The power plant at the lock houses well-maintained direct current generating equipment. Tours are provided of the power plant upon request.

The lock cut extends for a mile beyond the lock before rejoining the Oneida River approaching the village of Brewerton. Transient mooring is available along the north bank of the canal just after passing under Route 11. The Erie Canal traverses Oneida Lake to a point on the east shore of the lake between Sylvan Beach and Verona Beach State Park before continuing eastward toward Rome and Utica.

◆ ◆ ◆

Main Street, Brockport

PLACES TO SEE / THINGS TO DO

Low Bridge, Everybody Down

I've got an old mule and her name is Sal,
Fifteen years on the Erie Canal,
She's a good old worker and a good old pal,
Fifteen years on the Erie Canal.
We've filled some barges in our day,
Filled with lumber, coal, and hay—
And every inch of the way I know
From Albany to Buffalo.

Low bridge, everybody down,
Low bridge! We're coming to a town!
You can always tell your neighbor,
You can always tell your pal,
If you've ever navigated on the Erie Canal.

Oh! Where would I be if I lost my pal!
Fifteen years on the Erie Canal,
Oh, I'd like to see a mule as good as Sal,
Fifteen years on the Erie Canal.
A friend of mine got her sore,
Now he's got a broken jaw,
'Cause she let fly with her iron toe
And kicked him in to Buffalo.

by Thomas S. Allen

Sightseeing along the Erie Canal in the Finger Lakes Region

INFORMATION IS PROVIDED ABOUT PLACES TO SEE AND THINGS TO DO IN THE FINGER LAKES REGION ALONG A THIRTY-MILE-WIDE BAND WEST TO EAST ALONG THE ERIE CANAL. THIS BAND IS DIVIDED INTO TWO PARTS, A FIFTEEN-MILE-WIDE STRIP BETWEEN THE ERIE CANAL AND LAKE ONTARIO AND ANOTHER FIFTEEN-MILE-WIDE ZONE BETWEEN THE CANAL AND ROUTES 5 AND 20 ACROSS THE NORTHERN ENDS OF THE FINGER LAKES. INFORMATION ABOUT PLACES TO SEE AND THINGS TO DO IN ROCHESTER, THE WESTERN GATEWAY TO THE FINGER LAKES REGION, AND SYRACUSE, THE EASTERN GATEWAY TO THE FINGER LAKES REGION, CAN BE FOUND IN THE BOOK, *PERSONS, PLACES, AND THINGS AROUND THE FINGER LAKES REGION*.

Lake Ontario

Lake Ontario, the northern boundary of the region north of the Finger Lakes, is 193 miles long and 53 miles wide. With an area of 7,550 square miles, it is the smallest of the Great Lakes. It is 802 feet deep at its deepest point and contains 393 cubic miles of fresh water. The lake is elliptical in shape and is the easternmost of the Great Lakes. Although Lake Ontario is the smallest of the Great Lakes, it is not the shallowest; it is deeper than Lake Erie and Lake Huron. Its drainage area is 27,300 square miles—15,200 square miles in the United States and 12,100 in Canada.

Lake Ontario's shore line is regular and free of islands and navigational hazards except for the northeast section, which has diverse scenery with headlands and islands. The Thousand Islands Region is just east of the St. Lawrence River's entry into Lake Ontario.

Routes 5 and 20

Before the construction of the New York State Thruway in the 1950s, Routes 5 and 20 were the principal east-west highways north of the Finger Lakes. West to east, Routes 5 and 20 pass through the municipalities of Canandaigua, Geneva, Waterloo, Seneca Falls, and Auburn.

At Auburn, Route 5 proceeds northeast through the villages of Elbridge and Camillus to Syracuse. Route 20 continues eastward through the villages of Skaneateles and LaFayette through Onondaga County to Madison County. At LaFayette, Route 20 is intersected by Interstate 81, the north-south expressway between Syracuse and Binghamton.

Between Routes 5 and 20 and Lake Ontario—Description

The principal features of the area north of the Finger Lakes are the northern boundary, Lake Ontario, with its beautiful natural bays, Sodus Bay and Little Sodus Bay; the glacial-formed drumlins that dominate the landscape; and the Erie Canal that crosses the entire region. The New York State Thruway parallels the Erie Canal through the northern Finger Lakes Region. The Lake Ontario shoreline has scenic vistas created by erosion, particularly at Chimney Bluffs State Park.

The lake is one of the major influences on the weather in the region. The area is known for its fruit production, particularly apples, because of the moderating influence of Lake Ontario on the temperature.

The region contains one of the largest drumlin fields in the world. The field is bounded by Lake Ontario in the north and the Finger Lakes in the south; it extends from Syracuse in the east to about twenty-five miles west of Rochester. Drumlins, smooth ridges or hills of glacial drift, extend inland from Lake Ontario, both north into Canada and south into New York State. They were formed when the lake was the center of spreading Wisconsin Ice Age glaciers. Drumlins were molded by the movement of the ice above them and were elongated in the direction of the movement of the glacier.

The Erie Canal extends across the approximate north-south midpoint of the region north of the Finger Lakes, except at the northern end of Cayuga Lake where it bends southward and then curves back again to the north. From west to east, Rochester to Syracuse, the canal passes through the Wayne County villages of Macedon, Palmyra, Newark, Lyons, and Clyde, and north of the Cayuga County villages of Port Byron and Weedsport and the Onondaga County village of Jordan.

Between Routes 5 and 20 and Lake Ontario—Brief History

In June 1687 in Montreal, Marquis Denonville, the Governor of New France, assembled a military expedition comprised of 2,000 French army regulars and 600 Indian allies. The expedition traveled down the St. Lawrence River and across Lake Ontario to Irondequoit Bay in 200 bateaux and 200 canoes. Another force of 180 Frenchmen and over 300 Indians, commanded by La Durantaye and Tonty, joined the larger force at Irondequoit Bay. Denonville left 300 men to build a small fort to protect the canoes and barges, then marched overland to annihilate the Seneca Indians to reduce their competition with the French in the fur trade.

Denonville followed the Indian trail to Ganondagan, which was south of the present village of Victor. As he approached the major Seneca village through a ravine on July 13, 1867, his expedition was surprised by a Seneca ambush and was almost overwhelmed. Some of his Indian allies fled, but his Mohawk allies held. Denonville ordered the sounding of trumpets and the roll of drums, while executing a flanking movement to rout the Senecas. In retreating, the Senecas burned their village, but not their store of corn. Denonville's men tore down the Senecas' palisades, and completed the destruction.

One hundred Frenchmen and eighty Senecas were killed. Denonville's men burned three other Seneca villages and destroyed their stored corn and beans. His expedition then marched back to their boats at Irondequoit Bay and returned to Canada. No lasting benefit came to the French from this military venture. Ganondagan wasn't rebuilt; the Senecas merely moved farther inland, away from Lake Ontario. An adverse result for the French was that the Senecas were driven into alliances with the English.

The War of 1812, a war for which the fledgling United States was woefully unprepared, included skirmishes along the southern shore of Lake Ontario. President Madison's Secretary of the Navy chose Commodore Isaac Chancey to command the naval forces on the Great Lakes. Chancey was based at Sacket's Harbor at the eastern end of Lake Ontario, and that lake and Lake Erie were two of his major responsibilities. Chancey's British counterpart was Commodore Sir James Yeo.

At the beginning of the war, both Chauncey and Yeo had six ships on Lake Ontario; however, the Americans were outgunned thirty guns to one hundred. Chauncey's naval forces on Lake Ontario included the *Oneida* and the schooners *Conquest, Growler, Julia,* and *Pert*. Yeo's tactics were to cruise along the southern shore of Lake Ontario in his flagship, the *H.M.S. Royal George*, looking for undefended ports. He then seized the supplies stored there, either by force or by promising not to molest the settlers if they delivered their supplies willingly.

Five ships of Yeo's fleet were sighted off Sodus Point on June 19, 1813. The Redcoats landed from Yeo's ships and were opposed by sixty militia. The British seized the stores in the warehouses; however, most of the supplies had been hidden in nearby ravines. They burned all of the buildings in Sodus Point, except the Mansion House.

The British revisited the region on May 15, 1814, and went ashore in Pultneyville. General John Swift's militia was ready for the British when they landed, but he was persuaded to negotiate. Swift agreed to allow the British to take 100 barrels of flour from the local warehouse if the village was left alone. The highest quality flour had already been hidden in the woods. The *H.M.S. Royal George* fired a few cannonballs at the town as a parting gesture. The Selby house at the corner of Jay and Washington Street and the Legasse home at the bend in Lake Road were both struck by British cannonballs.

The building of the Erie Canal was the next major event in the region. As discussed in the Introduction, construction began to the east, at Rome, in 1817. In 1825, the Erie Canal was completed through the region north of the Finger Lakes from Albany to Buffalo; this opened up trade between the East and the Midwest. The canal was enlarged and upgraded in the mid-1800s, and again early in the twentieth century in an attempt to compete with the railroads. Initially, the railroads acted as feeders to the Erie Canal; eventually they went where the canals could not go. By 1850, rail transportation extended throughout the State.

Many short railroads were combined into one line across the State when the New York Central Railroad was formed in 1870. The Erie Railroad, completed in 1851, connected New York City with Dunkirk on Lake Erie via its roadbed across the southern tier of the State. Eventually, the railroads replaced the canal systems as the principal means of transporting both people and freight.

◆ ◆ ◆

Lock 30, Macedon

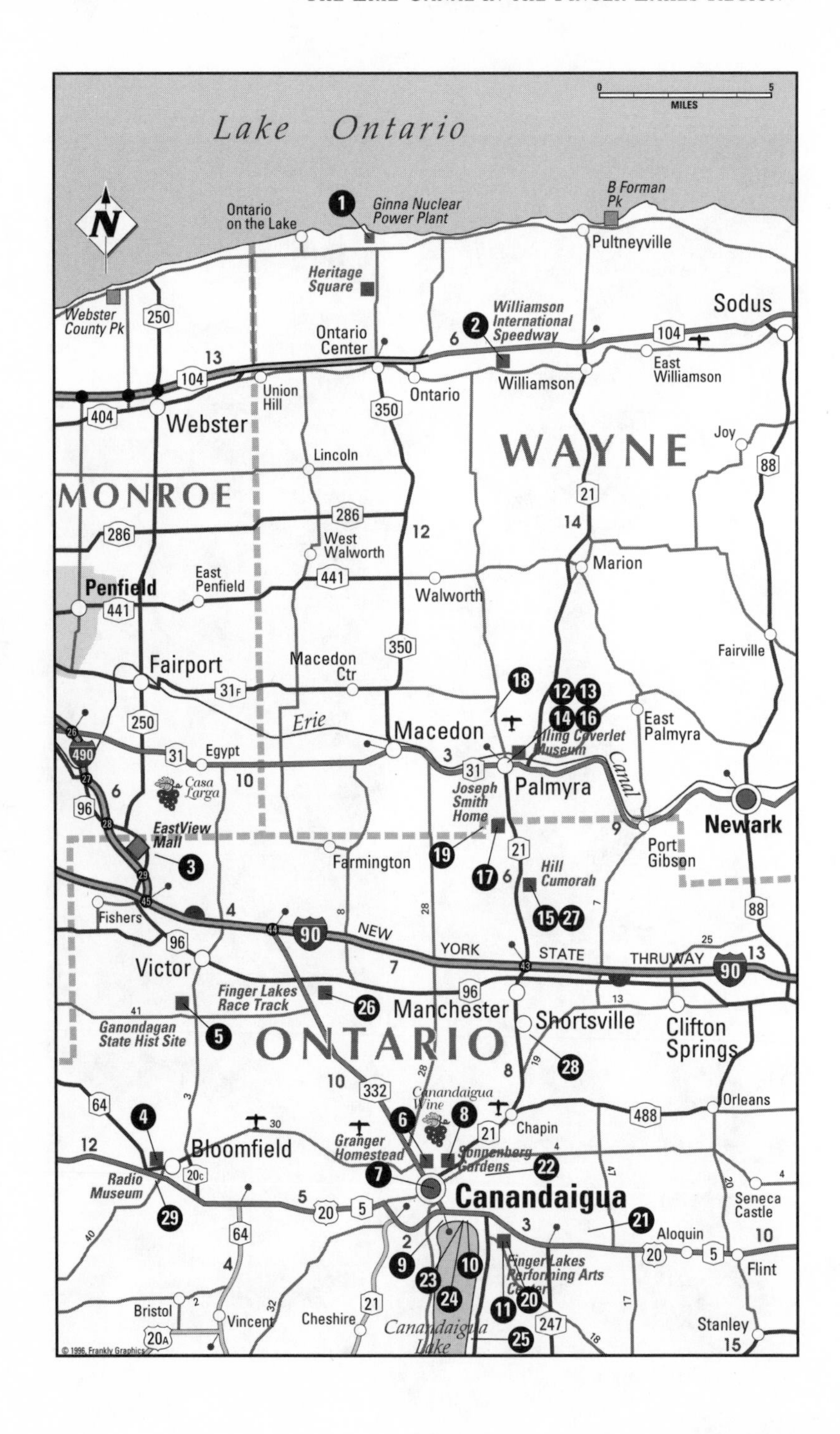

Lake Ontario
MILES
Ginna Nuclear Power Plant
Ontario on the Lake
B Forman Pk
Pultneyville
Heritage Square
Webster County Pk
Williamson International Speedway
Sodus
Ontario Center
East Williamson
Williamson
Ontario
Union Hill
Webster
WAYNE
Joy
Lincoln
MONROE
West Walworth
Marion
East Penfield
Penfield
Walworth
Fairville
Macedon Ctr
Fairport
Erie
Macedon
Egypt
Palmyra
East Palmyra
Canal
Casa Larga
Joseph Smith Home
EastView Mall
Newark
Farmington
Port Gibson
Hill Cumorah
Fishers
NEW YORK STATE THRUWAY
Victor
Finger Lakes Race Track
Manchester
Shortsville
Clifton Springs
Ganondagan State Hist Site
ONTARIO
Canandaigua Wine
Orleans
Chapin
Granger Homestead
Bloomfield
Sonnenberg Gardens
Radio Museum
Canandaigua
Seneca Castle
Aloquin
Finger Lakes Performing Arts Center
Flint
Bristol
Vincent
Cheshire
Canandaigua Lake
Stanley
© 1996, Frankly Graphics

• chapter four •

From Canandaigua to Lake Ontario

So pull in your towline,
And haul in the slack,
Take a reef in your britches,
And straighten your back.

But, whatever you do,
Don't ever forget
For to touch the mules gently
When the cook's on the deck.

The cook, she's a daisy,
She's dead gone on me;
She's got fiery red hair,
And she's sweet twenty-three.

—*Anonymous*

Canandaigua—Brief Description and History

Canandaigua, the county seat of Ontario County, is a city of over 12,000 at the northern end of Canandaigua Lake. It is the home of Sonnenberg Gardens, a beautiful garden estate with a 1887 Victorian mansion surrounded by nine gardens; the Finger Lakes Performing Arts Center, the summer home of the Rochester Philharmonic Orchestra on the campus of the Finger Lakes Community College; and the Finger Lakes Race Track, the only thoroughbred race track in central New York.

Other Canandaigua attractions include the Granger Homestead and Carriage Museum and the Ontario County Historical Society Museum. Canandaigua is the headquarters of the Canandaigua Wine Company, the second-largest winery in the United States. Only E. and J. Gallo of Modesto, California, is larger. The tasting room of the Canandaigua Wine Company is located on the grounds of Sonnenberg Gardens.

With its wide main street and stately homes, the city was chosen as the location of the land office of Nathaniel Gorham and Oliver Phelps in the 1700s. It was the most important municipality in the region before the Erie Canal and the New York Central Railroad shifted the economic expansion to the north, along a line from Syracuse to Rochester to Buffalo.

The present location of the Ontario County Courthouse in Canandaigua was the site of the signing of the the 1794 Treaty of Canandaigua (the Pickering Treaty), which established peace between the Six Nations of the Iroquois Confederacy and the young United States of America. Four of the six Iroquois Nations had sided with Great Britain during the Revolutionary War, and the Iroquois Confederacy was considering allying with the Indians of Ohio, who had defeated the first two expeditions President Washington sent west to subdue them. However, the victory of General "Mad" Anthony Wayne at Fallen Timbers checked the British-backed effort of the Indians in Ohio to prevent expansion of the United States westward.

The treaty defined Iroquois property rights, including the placement of a western boundary on their land, and reserved land for a military road along the Niagara River. Goods and a higher annuity were granted to the Indians, cementing the relationship so that the Iroquois fought against Great Britain in the War of 1812. Timothy Pickering signed the Treaty for the United States; Cornplanter, Farmer's Brother, Fish Carrier, Handsome Lake, Little Beard, Red Jacket, and forty-four others signed with crosses for the Iroquois.

At least two famous trials have been held in Canandaigua: that of Jemima Wilkinson, the leader of a religious sect, in 1799 for blasphemy, and that of Susan B. Anthony, the Women's Rights Movement leader, in 1873 for attempting to register to vote.

The charge of blasphemy was leveled at Jemima Wilkinson by James Parker, a magistrate of Ontario County, who had previously been a member of her religious sect. During the first attempt to serve her a warrant, she outrode the servers and escaped. At the second attempt, she and the women in her household workshop physically threw out the two servers, tearing their clothing. The third attempt was made by a posse of thirty men who surrounded her house at midnight; however, Dr. Fargo, who came with the posse, warned them that Jemima's health would not permit her to be taken into custody.

She agreed to appear before the next session of the Ontario County Circuit Court in Canandaigua. The case was presented to a grand jury, but, when the presiding judge ruled that blasphemy was not an indictable offense, her case was dismissed.

Susan B. Anthony registered to vote on November 1, 1872, and voted in the 1872 presidential election in Rochester. She was arraigned since the law granting women the right to vote had not yet been passed (and wouldn't be for another forty-eight years). Her trial was moved to Canandaigua since it was thought that she couldn't receive a fair trial in Rochester. When her trial began on June 17, 1873, her lawyer, Henry Selden, was surprised to see Judge Ward Hunt, a relatively inexperienced judge, on the bench. Hunt's mentor was the politically influential Roscoe Conkling, U.S. Senator from New York.

Henry Selden argued that Susan's only crime was that she was a woman, and that she believed that the fourteenth and fifteenth amendments had given her the right to vote. Following the District Attorney's argument that Susan had broken the law, Judge Hunt said that Susan was not granted the right to vote by the Constitution. He took a written note from his pocket and began to read to the jury: "If I am right in this, the result must be a verdict ... of guilty and I therefore direct that you find a verdict of guilty."

An incensed Selden demanded a retrial, which was denied by Judge Hunt. Susan refused to pay her $100 fine. Universal public opinion favored Susan, and the newspapers gave wide coverage to the miscarriage of justice in her case.

Two individuals who spent their youth, or at least part of it, in Canandaigua were Stephen A. Douglas and John Willys. Douglas was known for his participation in the Lincoln-Douglas debates when he and Abraham Lincoln were campaigning against each other for the U.S. Senate. Douglas attended the Canandaigua Academy in the early 1830s, before he moved to the Midwest and became a U.S. Senator from Illinois. He was active in the debating society at the Canandaigua Academy, polishing the skills with which he defeated Lincoln for the Senate seat.

John North Willys was born in Canandaigua in 1873 and became an entrepreneur at an early age. He was half-owner of a laundry at sixteen and made his early money in the bicycle business, grossing a half million a year by the time he was twenty-seven. He went into the automobile business in 1900 and eventually owned and ran the Willys-Overland Company, which subsequently was the manufacturer of the original Jeep.

In 1914, he turned down an offer of $80 million dollars for his share of Willys-Overland, but he hung on and added to his fortune in World War I. His fortunes waned in the recession after World War I, and he sold his share of the company for $20 million dollars in 1929. President Hoover appointed him Ambassador to Poland.

Willys died in New York City in 1935. His automobile company became a part of American Motors and then part of Chrysler Corporation, when American Motors was bought out by the third largest automobile manufacturer in the U.S.

NORTH OF THE CANAL

PLACES TO SEE

1) Robert E. Ginna Nuclear Power Plant

The Robert E. Ginna Nuclear Power Plant Unit 1, located sixteen miles east of Rochester on the south shore of Lake Ontario, is owned and operated by the Rochester Gas and Electric Corporation (RG&E). The Ginna station has a pressurized light-water reactor system that generates electricity through the use of nuclear energy. The nuclear steam system, rated at 515 gross (490 net) mw, was manufactured by the Westinghouse Corporation. The reactor system consists of three major components: the primary loop, the secondary loop, and the condensing cycle.

The reactor system is fueled with uranium in pellet form. The pellets are placed in zirconium fuel rods that are built into fuel assemblies. The reactor core contains 121 fuel assemblies, each containing 179 fuel rods, for a total of 21,659 rods. Each of two vertical shell, inverted U-tube steam generators has 3,260 tubes. The turbine generator is a three-element turbine rated at 496,322 kw.

Commercial operation of the Ginna Nuclear Power Plant began on June 1, 1970. RG&E conducts tours of Ginna station, but visitors must make arrangements in advance. Because of the obvious need for security, visitors must meet the following requirements:

- Tours must be arranged six weeks in advance with the RG&E Speakers and Tours Bureau.
- Only group tours (10 to 25 people) are given.
- No one under the age of eighteen is permitted in the Ginna plant. Simulator tours are provided in the training center for those under eighteen.
- All visitors must be citizens of the U.S. and must have some form of picture identification with them. Simulator tours can be provided for non-U.S. citizens.
- Names and addresses of visitors must be submitted to the RG&E Speakers and Tours Bureau at least one week before the tour.

THINGS TO DO

2) Williamson International Speedway

Williamson International Speedway, which is located two miles west of Williamson in Wayne County on Route 104, is a National Association for Stock Car Racing (NASCAR) track with a paved half-mile oval. Three divisions of stock car racing—Late Models, WIS Modifieds, and Street Stocks—are held on Friday nights from mid-May through mid-September. The track also features NHRA Drag Racing on Saturday nights.

SOUTH OF THE CANAL

PLACES TO SEE

West of Canandaigua

3) Valentown Museum of Local History

The Valentown Museum of Local History, located on Route 96 opposite Eastview Mall, was built in 1879 as a community center and shopping plaza. The Pittsburgh, Shawmut, and Northern Railroad planned a line from Pittsburgh to link up with the New York Central Railroad at Macedon; it was to compete with the Pennsylvania Railroad in carrying coal to the Great Lakes. The preliminary railroad survey showed that the new line would pass through Levi Valentine's farm, which was located just north of Victor.

Valentine laid out a new village with streets and building lots. He constructed a four-story frame building that was to be the center of the village. He named his village Valentown, a combination of his last name and the last name of his grandfather, Ichabod Town. Unfortunately, the raiload went bankrupt after reaching Wayland, and did not extend as far north as Valentine's farm. However, the Valentown building became a center of business and rural social life in the area.

The basement of the building was used as stabling for visitors' horses. The first floor included a grocery store, meat market, harness maker's shop, cobbler's shop, bakery, and a community room, which provided a meeting place for church and social groups. The second floor housed the grange room, art school, theatrical school, business school, and the school of music for members of the fifty-four-piece Valentown band. The most well-known graduate of the theatrical school was Jessie Bonesteele in 1882. She trained Melvin Douglas and Catherine Cornell for her traveling stock company. The third floor has an 18-foot ceiling with four chandeliers and a full stage at one end. It was used for concerts, dances, church services, and plays.

The use of the Valentown Building declined early in the 1900s. After the Grand Military Balls of the hamlet of Fishers' Home Defense were held there in 1917-18, the building was closed. The building was vacant for over twenty years. Historian Sheldon Fisher, whose great-grandfather founded the nearby hamlet of Fishers in 1811, purchased the property in 1940 to restore it. The Valentown Musem has been restored to look as the building did over 100 years ago. Many of the artifacts displayed were originally used there. Museum exhibits include:

- Displays of Indian artifacts from Ganondagan, Seneca capital in Victor from 1650-87
- Items from the 1687 battle between Denonville's French Army and the Senecas
- Artifacts and documents of the Phelps-Gorham Purchase of western New York in 1788
- Original interior of the Auburn and Rochester Railroad station in Fishers
- Civil War memorabilia from area soldiers
- Haberdashery and millinery shops with a display of many hats and molds
- Artifacts from the Mormon leader Brigham Young's local 1829 home and mill site
- The original country store as it was in the 1800s
- Early musical instruments and sheet music
- Pioneer hand tools and farm implements

The Valentown Museum is open from Wednesday through Sunday, May 1 through October 31. A nominal admission fee is charged.

4) Electronic Communications Museum

The Antique Wireless Association Electronic Communications Museum is housed in the restored 1838 Academy Building on Routes 5 and 20 in East Bloomfield. The museum contains one of the largest collections of radio apparatus associated with the early pioneers, such as DeForest, Edison, and Marconi. Displays in the museum include:

- A "cat's whisker" radio
- Marconi wireless apparatus
- Nineteenth century telephones
- Working model of world's first wireless apparatus
- Shipboard wireless transmitters
- A fully-stocked 1925 radio store
- Western Union Telegraph Office
- An early Telsa spark coil in operation
- First radio and television tubes
- Atwater Kent and Stromberg Carlson radios
- A two-inch television screen
- An early broadcast studio

The museum also has a modern amateur radio station, W2AN.

The Antique Wireless Association, founded in 1952, was chartered as a nonprofit corporation by the State of New York. The association, a member of the American Association of Museums and the Regional Conference of Historical Agencies, is devoted to research and documentation of the history of wireless communications. The museum is open Sunday afternoons from May through October, and Saturday afternoons and Wednesday evenings from June through August. It is closed on holidays. No admission is charged.

5) Ganondagan State Historic Site

The Ganondagan State Historic Site, which is located at 1488 Victor-Holcomb Road in Victor, is the site of a major Seneca Indian town and palisaded granary. The Senecas stored hundreds of thousands of bushels of corn in the granary, which was built on a mesa; they used it as a fort when they were attacked. The town and its Boughton Hill burial grounds were designated a National Historic Landmark in 1964. The Marquis Denonville, Governor General of New France, led a campaign against the Iroquois in July 1687 to destroy the Seneca Nation and to eliminate their competition in the fur trade. His forces destroyed the granary at Fort Hill as they swept through the region. The restored granary was placed in the National Register of Historic Places in 1966.

The historic site has three trails marked with illustrated signs: Earth is our Mother Trail, Trail of Peace on Boughton Hill, and Granary Trail on Fort Hill. The visitor center, which has an audiovisual program, research archives, and special seasonal events, is open daily from mid-May through Labor Day and Wednesday through Sunday between Labor Day and the end of October. The trails are open year-round during daylight hours. Admission is free; reservations may be made for group tours. The visitor center and some of the trails are accessible to the handicapped.

Canandaigua

6) Granger Homestead and Carriage Museum

The Granger Homestead, located on a twelve-acre site at 295 North Main Street, Canandaigua, is a federal-style mansion completed in 1816. The mansion, which contains detailed carved moldings and mantelpieces, took two years to build at a cost of $13,000. Almost half of the twenty-three rooms have been restored.

Many of the furnishings on display in the restored period rooms were owned by four generations of the Granger family. The period furniture includes the dining room table that Dolly Madison saved when the British Army burned the White House during the War of 1812. Upon request, visitors are shown a thirty-minute TV documentary, "The Statesman from Canandaigua," about Gideon Granger, the homestead's builder.

The Carriage Museum contains over fifty horse-drawn vehicles, including coaches, fire-fighting equipment, hearses, sleighs, sporting vehicles, and commercial wagons. The carriages were built in the period from 1820 to 1939, and many have been restored to their original condition. The collection includes the half-moon carriage used by Jemima Wilkinson, "Publick Universal Friend," leader of a religious sect near Branchport during the late 1700s and early 1800s.

Gideon Granger was a Yale graduate, a lawyer, a Connecticut State Senator, father of the public school system in Connecticut, and the U.S. Postmaster General from 1800 until 1813, in the administrations of Thomas Jefferson and James Madison. Granger became familiar with the Finger Lakes Region when he was the agent for the State of Connecticut in settling Oliver Phelps' estate.

Granger moved to Canandaigua after he left Madison's administration, practiced law, and served a term as a New York State Senator. He died in 1822. His son, Francis, ran unsuccessfully for Vice President and served as Postmaster General in the abbreviated term of President William Henry Harrison.

The Granger Homestead served as the Granger Place School for Young Ladies from 1875 to 1906. The Granger family lived at the homestead until 1930, when Miss Antoinette Granger, the last of the Granger family, passed away. The homestead, which is maintained by the Granger Homestead Society, is open Tuesday through Saturday afternoons from mid-May through mid-October. Additional summer hours are Sunday afternoons from June 1 through August 31.

Granger Homestead, Canandaigua

7) Ontario County Historical Society Museum

The Ontario County Historical Society Museum, located at 55 North Main Street, Canandaigua, was constructed in 1914 to preserve the county's unique heritage. The museum features a series of thematic exhibits, a "hands-on" Discovery Center, and a research library on local history. The Ontario County Historical Society sponsors lectures, preservation activities, educational programs, special events, and a permanent exhibit on the history of Ontario County.

8) Sonnenberg Gardens and Mansion

Sonnenberg Gardens and Mansion, at 151 Charlotte Street in Canandaigua, is a fifty-acre estate that includes nine formal gardens, a greenhouse conservatory, ponds, statuary, and a forty-room mansion built by Mr. and Mrs. Frederick Ferris Thompson in 1887. The architecture of the rusticated gray stone mansion, trimmed in red Medina sandstone, is a blend of Elizabethan, Richardson Romanesque, and Tudor influences. Designed by Boston architect Francis Allen, the mansion has a prominent turret, half-timbered gables, and a covered carriage entranceway.

The Palm House is the centerpiece of the greenhouse complex and is constructed of 1,100 pieces of curved, frosted glass. The Peach House, which contains its original iron trellises, is now the Peach House luncheon restaurant. The mansion houses two gift shops, and the Canandaigua Wine Company operates its wine tasting room on the grounds of the estate.

The Thompsons purchased the property in 1863 from the Holberton family, who had named the house Sonnenberg (Sunny Hill) for a small town in Germany. The Thompsons retained the name, but replaced the house. Mrs. Thompson commissioned Ernest W. Bowditch, highly regarded Boston horticulturist and landscape gardener, to design and oversee the construction of the gardens.

Bowditch's earlier accomplishments were the private gardens of Cornelius Vanderbilt and Pierre Lorillard, and the park system in Cleveland, Ohio. At Sonnenburg, he designed nine separate gardens, an aviary, and a deer park. A tenth garden, a beautiful

Japanese garden, was designed by landscape architect K. Wadamori.

The Italian Garden is laid out in four large rectangles containing silver and red fleur-de-lis arrangements bordered by seventy-two hand-trimmed, cone-shaped yews. Adjacent to the Italian garden is the Blue and White Garden, called the "intimate" garden by Mrs. Thompson. Privacy is ensured in this garden, planted only with blue flowers and white flowers, by walls of hedges and vines.

The Pansy Garden, bordered by a wall of yews and a tall stone banquette, is accessed via an archway in the hedge from the Blue and White Garden, which is directly in front of it. The Pansy Garden, designed as a place for meditation and reflection, has a six-foot-high fountain that flows into a marble birdbath shaped like a pansy. The small Moonlight Garden, behind a row of cherry dogwood and bordered with privet hedges adjacent to the Pansy Garden, was planted with fragrant white flowers to be enjoyed by moonlight.

The Sub-Rosa or "Hidden" Garden, containing arborvitae, English ivy, juniper, lilacs, privet, and trumpet vine, is surrounded by dense, square-clipped boxwood hedges. This garden, viewed as an "outdoor chapel," contains a fountain, a pool, four white marble busts of the seasons, and two marble lions. The Rose Garden is planted with over 2,600 white, pink, and red roses; the Old-Fashioned (Colonial) Garden is known for its variety of color. The Rock Garden has a stone lookout tower, shady wooded pathways, and a water cascade.

The Japanese Garden has brooks and lily ponds spanned by small bridges, two stone devil dogs (one smiling to greet friends, another scowling to fend off evil spirits), and a large bronze statue of Buddha, sitting in the lotus position. This garden has English yews and many varieties of trees, including bronze Japanese maples, Japanese umbrella trees, and red cedars.

Mrs. Thompson outlived her husband by twenty-four years; she died in 1923. The estate was sold to the U.S. Goverment, which built a Veterans Administration hospital on the estate's farmlands and converted the mansion into nurses' quarters. Sonnenberg Gardens, Inc., a nonprofit educational corporation, was chartered by a act of Congress in 1972 to preserve the mansion and gardens for display to the public. Sonnenberg Gardens is open daily from May through October.

9) Canandaigua Lake State Marine Park

Canandaigua Lake State Marine Park, located off South Main Street in Canandaigua at the northern end of the Lake, has boat launch facilities, a comfort station, and parking space for over 200 cars and trailers.

10) Kershaw Park

Kershaw Park, a City of Canandaigua park located on seven acres at the northern end of Canandaigua Lake, has a supervised swimming area with a floating swim dock, a small craft launch area, and a first aid station. The park also contains a picnic area with barbecue grills, a sand pit volleyball court, grassy play areas, and seasonal rest rooms.

John "Jack" Kershaw, a member of the Board of Health and Public Safety for whom the park is named, suggested that a park be constructed on the site in 1920. In 1931, Dr. Charles Booth promoted the implementation of Jack Kershaw's recommendation. Construction of the park became a Works Progress Administration project during the Depression; the State provided the labor and the City furnished the trucks and materials. The park was officially opened on August 11, 1936.

11) Finger Lakes Community College

Finger Lakes Community College, founded in 1965 as a unit of the State University of New York, is located on a 235-acre campus at 4355 Lake Shore Drive, just east of Canandaigua. It is a two-year coeducational college with approximately 4,000 students; it awards about 500 degrees and certificates each year.

The multilevel terraced campus houses classrooms, administration and faculty offices, a gymnasium, laboratories, a library and educational resource center, and a student union. The college has three extension sites: the Geneva Center, the Wayne County Extension Center in the Maple Building of the Newark Developmental Center, and the Victor Center at the Victor Senior High School.

A $7,200,000 addition was built at the college in 1991. The Finger Lakes Performing Arts Center, the summer home of the Rochester Philharmonic Orchestra, is located on the campus of the Finger Lakes Community College.

Palmyra

12) Alling Coverlet Museum

The Alling Coverlet Musuem, located at 122 William Street in Palmyra, houses the largest collection of coverlets in the United States. The museum, which is administered by Historic Palmyra, Inc., contains coverlets collected by Mrs. Harold Alling for over thirty years. The museum is located in a two-story brick building donated by Mrs. Henry Griffith.

One of the notable coverlets on display is the woven coverlet "American Tapestry," an approximately eighty-inches by ninety-inches bed cover woven of homespun wool and linen. Coverlets were made to be used, but they were also heirlooms. The flax and wool were raised by the early pioneers, cleaned, sorted, and spun prior to weaving the coverlet. Dyes were made from local flowers, roots, and weeds.

Most coverlets were made by professional weavers. Two of the best in the mid-1800s were Ira Hadsell and James Van Ness. Professional weavers wove in geometric patterns; they sometimes used as many as twenty-four harnesses. Later, they used the French Jacquard loom controlled by punched cards to make more complicated patterns. Coverlets made by housewives were usually made on four-harness looms, using the overshot weave.

Historic Palmyra, Inc., operates a gift shop in the coverlet museum that offers handcrafted items and books about textiles. The Alling Coverlet Museum is open afternoons from June through mid-October and at other times by appointment.

Historic Palmyra, Inc. is a nonprofit organization dedicated to community service, historic preservation, and the operation of the Alling Coverlet Museum, the Palmyra Historical Museum, and the William Phelps General Store Museum.

13) Palmyra Historical Museum

The Palmyra Historical Museum, located at 132 Market Street, houses antiques, children's toys, Palmyra memorabilia, and Victorian period rooms. The museum takes visitors back to an earlier time when Palmyra was a manufacturing center that used the Erie Canal to transport products, including agricultural implements, carriages, printing press equipment, and sleighs.

14) William Phelps General Store Museum

The William Phelps General Store Museum, located at 140 Market Street, is furnished with original Phelps family artifacts. The museum provides a snapshot of a 1890s general store.

15) Hill Cumorah and the Moroni Monument

The brochure,"Welcome to Historic Mormon Country," contains the following explanation of Hill Cumorah, four miles south of Palmyra:

> In A.D. 421, Moroni, the last survivor of a great civilization that inhabited the Americas from 600 B.C. to A.D. 420, buried in this hill a set of gold plates on which was recorded the history of his people. By commandment of God, Moroni returned as an angel and delivered the plates to Joseph Smith in 1827. Joseph Smith translated the plates as the Book of Mormon, a companion scripture to the Bible. The Book of Mormon tells of the visit of Jesus Christ to the ancient Americans.

Hill Cumorah and Moroni Monument, south of Palmyra

Hill Cumorah is a prominent drumlin, formed by glacial activity, in the region north of the Finger Lakes. It is the site of a spectacular outdoor religious pageant, *America's Witness for Christ*, performed each summer by a cast of over 600 for audiences of 100,000 people. The significance of Hill Cumorah is explained through exhibits, paintings, and video presentations in the Visitor Center, which is open year-round. Free guided tours are conducted daily.

16) Historic Grandin Building

The Historic Grandin Building on Main Street in Palmyra was constructed in 1828, three years after the completion of the Erie Canal. E. B. Grandin supervised the printing of the first edition of the Book of Mormon in 1830. This first edition consisted of 5,000 leather-bound 590-page copies. The visitor center is open year-round; it offers free displays, films, and guided tours.

17) Joseph Smith Home

Joseph Smith, the first president of the Church of Jesus Christ of Latter-day Saints, and his father and brothers built this frame house in Palmyra in 1820. He lived in the house from his nineteenth to his twenty-second year. The homestead, located south of Route 31 and west of Route 21, has been restored to its original condition with period furnishings. The visitor center has free displays, films, and guided tours year-round.

18) Martin Harris Farm

Martin Harris was an early follower of Joseph Smith and a strong believer in the Book of Mormon. He mortgaged his farm to finance the first edition of the Book of Mormon, which was printed at the historic E. B. Grandin Building in 1830.

An 1850 Erie Canal cobblestone house is now located on the former Harris farm on Church Street in Palmyra. The visitor center is open year-round; it has displays, films, and free guided tours.

19) The Sacred Grove

The Sacred Grove, located south of Route 31 and west of the Joseph Smith Home in Palmyra, was the site of a visitation at which Joseph Smith learned from Heavenly Beings that he should join no established church.

When Joseph Smith was fourteen, he wondered which of the local churches he should join. He noted a passage in the Bible, James 1:5, "If any lack wisdom, let him ask of God." He walked westward from his home on a beautiful spring morning into a grove of trees nearby. He knelt in prayer in the grove and had a vision: "I saw a pillar of light. When the light rested upon me, I saw two personages, whose brightness and glory defy all description, standing above me in the air. One of them spoke unto me, calling me by name and said, pointing to the other, 'This is my Beloved Son; hear him.' "

Seven years later he was directed to the gold plates, buried in Hill Cumorah, from which he translated the Book of Mormon.

THINGS TO DO

Canandaigua

20) Finger Lakes Performing Arts Center

The Finger Lakes Performing Arts Center, the summer home of the Rochester Philharmonic Orchestra, is located on the campus of the Finger Lakes Community College at 4355 Lakeshore Drive, off Routes 5 and 20, about a mile east of Canandaigua. The amphitheatre opened in 1983. Indoor seating is available, in addition to lawn seats outside the shell. Concert-goers bring lawn chairs and blankets, and sit on the hillside overlooking the amphitheatre. Picnicking is allowed on the grounds surrounding the shell; refreshments are available at the Performing Arts Center.

A light classics series of concerts is offered on Saturday evenings during the summer. Two annual events are a July 4th Family Day Concert with fireworks and an 1812 Overture concert, complete with cannons and fireworks. Sunday Evening Pops Concerts are scheduled every summer, as well as rock concerts and many other performances.

21) New York Pageant of Steam

The Annual Pageant of Steam, which began in 1961, is held in early August on Gehan Road in Hopewell, off Routes 5 and 20, three miles east of Canandaigua. Steam engines are demonstrated sawing lumber and threshing grain, and steam traction engines and tractors participate in daily parades. The three-day event also includes a display of over 600 gasoline engines and over 200 early gasoline-engine powered tractors.

The pageant features daily parades, wagon rides, steam whistle concerts, and a flea market. Live bands play on several nights. Antique tractor pulls are scheduled for all three evenings. In a recent year, over 12,000 visitors attended the pageant. Campsites with shower facilities are available on the grounds.

22) Canandaigua Speedway

The Canandaigua Speedway, located at the Ontario County Fairgrounds, is a DIRT (Drivers' Independent Race Track) track. Races are held Saturday evenings, and selected other evenings, from early April through August.

23) Boat Rides on The Canandaigua Lady

The *Canandaigua Lady*, which can accommodate 150 passengers (130 for dining) on its upper deck and in its lower cabin, is a replica of a nineteenth-century paddlewheel steamboat. The vessel has a beam of twenty-four feet and a length of eighty-eight feet, or one hundred feet if the gang plank at the bow and the paddlewheel at the stern are included in the measurement.

The lower cabin is air conditioned and has full bar service, a dance floor, and rest rooms. The *Canandaigua Lady* offers dinner cruises, lunch cruises, supper cruises, a Sunday brunch, Sunday breakfast, and narrated boat tours.

Many special event cruises are available, including anniversary cruises, birthday cruises, corporate charters, a fall foliage cruise, fund raisers, field trips, private charters, school party cruises, tour groups, moonlight cruises, and wedding cruises. The ticket office for the *Canandaigua Lady* is located at 169 Lakeshore Drive, Canandaigua.

24) Captain Gray's Boat Tours

Captain Gray's Boat Tours, which began service in 1972, offers narrated tours of Canandaigua Lake daily from late morning until mid-evening from the Inn on the Lake dock at the foot of Main Street in Canandaigua. Captain Gray's Boat Tours offers one-hour, two-hour, and around-the-lake cruises as well as specialty cruises for events such as bridal and baby showers, group meetings, family and class reunions, and wedding rehearsals.

25) Thendara Inn— Historic Restaurant and Inn

Thendara is located four miles south of the city of Canandaigua on Route 364 (East Lake Road) on Canandaigua Lake. The fourteen-room Victorian house was built in 1900 by John Raines, State Senator, U.S. Congressman, and Republican leader of Ontario County. Thendara, a Mohawk Indian word meaning "the meeting place," was built on a bluff on thirty-five acres overlooking Deep Run Cove. Raines was known as the sponsor of "Raines Law," which increased the tax on all hotels that served liquor and specified that only hotels, not bars and restaurants, could serve liquor on Sunday.

The Canandaigua Yacht Club purchased Thendara from the Raines family; it was used as their clubhouse and base for sailing events for many years. C. J. "Jimmie" Miller purchased Thendara in 1975 and converted it into an inn and restaurant. Thendara was renovated in 1988; care was taken to preserve the architectural details of the early 1900s. The country inn has three dining rooms: the Victorian Room, with ceiling beams, a fireplace, and wainscoting; the Longview Room; and the Veranda, with its spectacular views of Canandaigua Lake.

The Inn has guest rooms furnished with turn-of-the-century antiques. One suite features a skylit jacuzzi. Thendara accommodates tour groups as well as weddings and receptions, and provides catering at other locations. The restaurant can accommodate over sixty people, depending on the seating arrangement, for conferences and retreats. Thendara has a par three golf course, the Lakeside Links.

Between Canandaigua and the Canal

26) Finger Lakes Race Track

Finger Lakes Race Track, located in Farmington at the intersection of Routes 96 and 332, about six miles north of Canandaigua, opened on May 23, 1962. The Track offers an over 170-day thoroughbred racing season. Hall of Fame jockeys, including Steve Cauthen, Angel Cordero, and Bill Shoemaker have ridden at the Finger Lakes Race Track.

Finger Lakes Race Track offers an average of ten races per day from early April until the first week of December. The major races include the Finger Lakes Breeders' Cup, the New York Oaks, the New York Derby, and the New York Breeders' Futurity. Total wagering in 1995 was over $172,000,000.

Concession stands are located throughout the facility, and a limited menu with table seating is available in the Paddock Room. A full luncheon menu is offered in the air-conditioned, glass-enclosed Terrace Dining Room. Parking for the handicapped is near the clubhouse entrance, and handicapped access to all levels is provided via an elevator in the lower grandstand.

27) The Hill Cumorah Pageant

The Hill Cumorah Pageant is held in mid-July at Hill Cumorah, four miles south of Palmyra on Route 21. Recognized as America's largest outdoor drama, the Pageant is attended annually by over 100,000 people from around the world.

It is based on the Book of Mormon and tells the story of the rise and fall of an ancient civilization on this continent between 600 BC and AD 400.

The pageant features a cast of 600, 1400 costumes, and a high-tech digital sound recording of the Mormon Tabernacle Choir and a 100-voice children's choir with the Utah Symphony Orchestra in the Salt Lake City Tabernacle. The pageant has attention-getting special effects, such as explosions, fireballs, volcanoes, and a prophet burned at the stake. Staging includes fifteen-foot water curtains, a quality outdoor sound system, and thirty- and fifty-foot light towers using more than 500,000 watts of power.

Critics have made the following observations of the pageant:

- "A pageant performed with the spirit of a George Lucas techno-dazzler and the scope of a Cecil B. DeMille epic."—The New York *Times*
- "Staging the Mormon Pageant on this holy site, with the statue of Moroni glittering atop the hill, roughly equals staging Oberammergau at Lourdes, except that this show has a distinctly American-style flash and grandeur."—Rochester *Democrat and Chronicle*
- "One of the most dramatic moments in the production takes place when the resurrected Christ appears 30 feet in the air and slowly descends to the highest point of the gigantic seven-level stage."—The Buffalo *News*
- "As always, the pageant promises glittering exotic costumes and an extensive sound and light show."—Denver *Post*

The Hill Cumorah Pageant, which is one hour and fifteen minutes long, has been presented by the Church of Jesus of Latter-day Saints since 1937. The performance begins at dusk. No admission is charged, parking is free, and seating is provided for over 8,000 (or bring blankets or lawn chairs). Interpreters are provided for the hearing impaired, and French, German, and Spanish earphone translations are available.

28) The Wild Water Derby

The first annual Wild Water Derby sponsored by the Twin Cities (Manchester and Shortsville) Lions Club was held in April 1976. The Derby is held on three and a quarter miles of whitewater of the Canadaigua Lake outlet between Littleville and Manchester, on Route 21 south of the New York State Thruway. This stretch of the outlet is whitewater rapids for only a few days in the early spring, when the floodgates between Canandaigua Lake and the outlet are opened to reduce the high lake level. When the lake level has dropped and the floodgates are closed, the course provides an easy canoe trip. Later in the summer, the water is too low for good canoeing.

However, in early April, the whitewater over the course of the derby is rated Class III, and is possibly Class IV at the peak rapids at Shortsville. Classification of rapids varies from Class I (easy) to Class IV (possible risk to life). In his book written over forty years ago, *Canoeable Waterways of New York State*, canoeing authority Lawrence Grinnell described the stretch of the outlet used for the Derby:

> Just before the bridge at Littleville, one and one-half miles above Shortsville, is a partly destroyed dam, which still backs up water. Below this dam are impassable cataracts. Between Littleville and Manchester, the stream descends sharply from a plateau in a succession of steep, boulder-strewn rapids, some definitely too shallow, or otherwise impossible to run at this stage. Steep banks make line-downs impractical. The descent could be dangerous at high water. The stream is still too steep and rocky to put in at Manchester bridge and re-embark one-quarter mile below this bridge, thus making the total portage from Littleville of about three and one-quarter miles.

There are five classes of Derby participants:

- kayaks (the smallest class)
- two-man canoe—men's class
- mixed canoe class—male-female or all-female teams
- inflatables—plastic and rubber manufactured craft and inner-tube rafts
- homemade rafts

The fifth class, homemade rafts, has the most variety—from well-built craft to, on one occasion, a platform tied to fifty-gallon barrels that originally contained apple concentrate from South America. Beer barrels, casks, and kegs are also used as flotation devices. Some participants pay great attention to the artistic quality of the raft. Entries have included a craft decorated as a sea monster with a crew dressed as Vikings.

Personal flotation devices (life jackets) are required for all entrants, and kayakers must wear helmets. Many entrants wear wet suits. The derby is the principal fundraising event for the Twin Cities Lions Club. The awards committee provides trophies for the three fastest entrants in each category. Time to complete the race ranges from twenty minutes to just under thirty minutes.

29) Holloway House—Historic Restaurant

The Holloway House is located on Routes 5 and 20, eight miles west of Canandaigua. The colonial house, which was built by Peter Holloway in 1808, was a tavern and a stagecoach stop on the post road that became Routes 5 and 20. The restaurant has a relaxed atmosphere that is reminiscent of a Norman Rockwell painting.

The Holloway House specializes in American fare such as fried chicken, baked ham, lamb chops, roast turkey, and seafood. The Saturday night special is prime rib of beef. Bread and rolls are a specialty of the house, particularly the light Sally Lunn bread and the home-style orange rolls. The restaurant is also known for its desserts and its extensive wine cellar.

◆ ◆ ◆

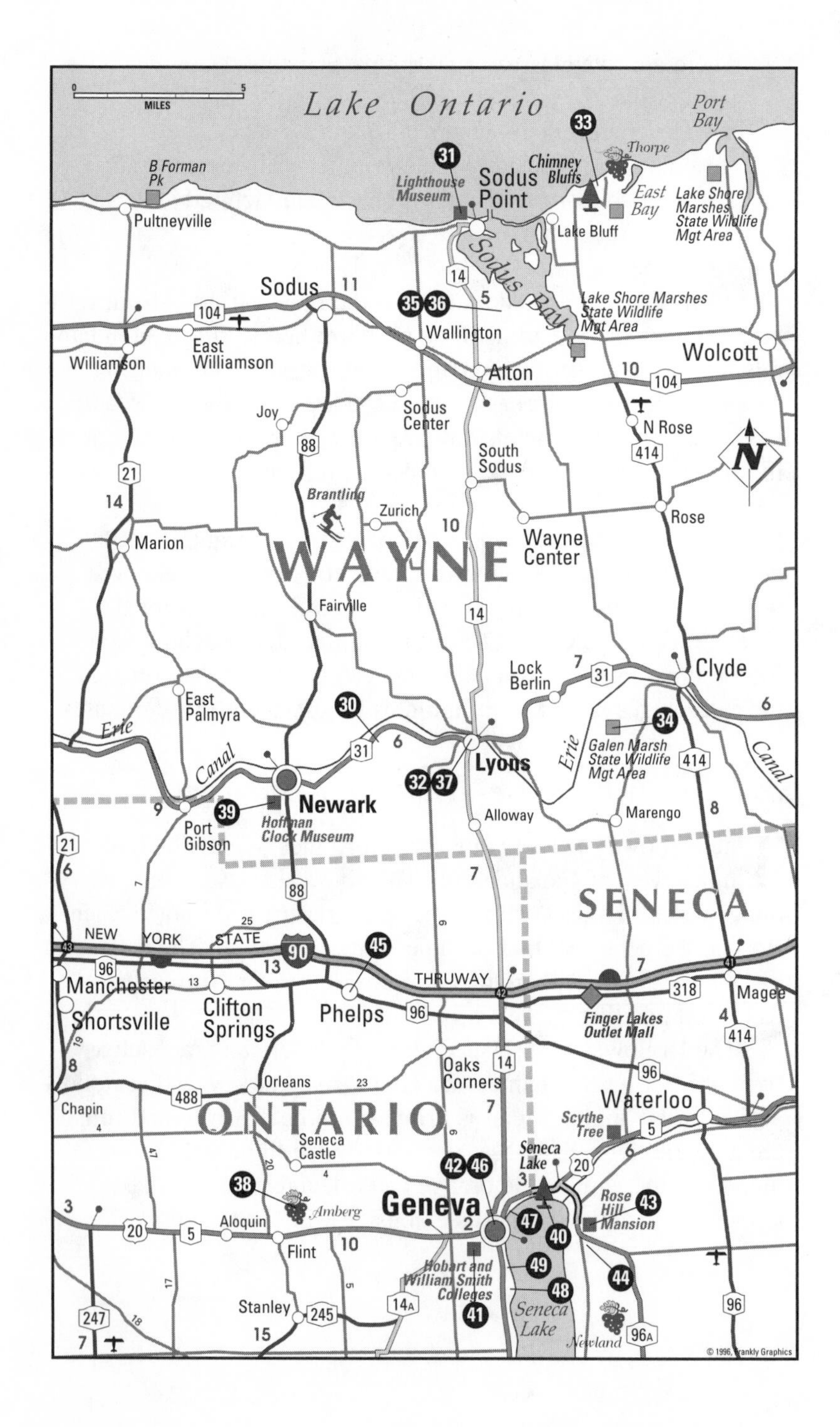
Lake Ontario
MILES
Port Bay
B Forman Pk
Lighthouse Museum
Sodus Point
Chimney Bluffs
Thorpe
East Bay
Lake Shore Marshes State Wildlife Mgt Area
Pultneyville
Lake Bluff
Sodus Bay
Sodus
Wallington
Williamson
East Williamson
Alton
Wolcott
Joy
Sodus Center
N Rose
South Sodus
Brantling
Zurich
Rose
Marion
WAYNE
Wayne Center
Fairville
Lock Berlin
Clyde
East Palmyra
Erie Canal
Lyons
Galen Marsh State Wildlife Mgt Area
Newark
Hoffman Clock Museum
Port Gibson
Alloway
Marengo
SENECA
NEW YORK STATE THRUWAY
Manchester
Shortsville
Clifton Springs
Phelps
Finger Lakes Outlet Mall
Magee
Oaks Corners
Orleans
Chapin
Waterloo
ONTARIO
Scythe Tree
Seneca Castle
Seneca Lake
Amberg
Geneva
Rose Hill Mansion
Aloquin
Flint
Hobart and William Smith Colleges
Stanley
Seneca Lake
Newland
© 1996, Frankly Graphics

• *chapter five* •

From Geneva to Lake Ontario

Then there's the state of New York,

Where some are very rich,

Themselves and a few others have dug a mighty ditch,

To render it more easy for us to find a way,

And sail upon the waters to Michigania;

Yea, yea, yea, to Michigania.

From the state song of the Wolverines

Geneva—Brief Description and History

Geneva, a city of over 15,000 at the northern end of Seneca Lake at the junction of Route 14 and Routes 5 and 20, is six miles south of New York State Thruway Exit 42. South Main Street is a street of stately homes and centuries-old trees; it was the center of the aristocracy of early Geneva. Pulteney Square and Trinity Episcopal Church, the oldest Episcopal church in western New York, give the street an old-world look. Hobart College extends along the street. Many of the multiple-level homes back up to Seneca Lake.

In addition to Hobart College, the oldest college in western New York, Geneva is the home of William Smith College and the New York State Agricultural Experiment Station. Two state parks are nearby: Seneca Lake State Park in Geneva and Sampson State Park, twelve miles south of the city on the east side of Seneca Lake. Some additional Geneva attractions include the Prouty-Chew Museum, Rose Hill Mansion, and the Smith Opera House for the Performing Arts.

Geneva is on the general site of the Seneca Indian village called Kanadesaga. It was a village of fifty homes, with cultivated fields and orchards, centered on the grounds of the present location of the New York State Agricultural Experiment Station. In 1756, Sir William Johnson, the British Superintendent of Indian Affairs, had an oak and pine stockade constructed at the site. With the exception of Jemima Wilkinson's religious colony, which subsequently moved to Keuka Lake, Geneva is the oldest non-Native American settlement in western New York.

A surveyor's error prevented Geneva from playing an even more important role in the development of western New York. The original Royal Charter of Massachusetts provided that state with a claim to the lands of western New York. To settle the claim dispute between the two states, both states agreed to a Pre-emption Line from Sodus Bay on Lake Ontario south along Seneca Lake to the Pennsylvania line.

The first survey of the Pre-emption Line, which defined the border of Massachusetts' pre-emptive rights (to sell the land), placed the line slightly to the west of Geneva. This caused Oliver Phelps, who with Nathaniel Gorham purchased the land from

Massachusetts, to build his land office at Canandaigua instead of Geneva, his original choice.

The first medical degree awarded to a woman in modern times was awarded to Elizabeth Blackwell in 1849 by Geneva College, which became Hobart College in 1851. The Medical School of Geneva College was founded in 1834 and was located in Geneva until it was moved to Syracuse in 1872. Elizabeth had been rejected by twenty-eight medical schools before being accepted by the Medical School of Geneva College. She was graduated first in her class on January 23, 1849.

Elizabeth founded both a medical college that was incorporated into Cornell Medical Center and an infirmary in New York, which is now the New York Infirmary-Beekman Downtown Hospital. The first women's residence hall at Hobart-William Smith Colleges was named Blackwell House in her honor, when it was built in 1899.

NORTH OF THE CANAL

PLACES TO SEE

30) Blue Cut Nature Center

Blue Cut Nature Center, which is located just west of Lyons, is a wildlife refuge and nature study center spread over more than forty acres of meadow, swamp, woodland, and drumlins (hills or ridges of glacial drift). Blue Cut has been the name of the locale since railroad tracks were built through the area in 1853. A cut made through a drumlin revealed Vernon Shale that had a bluish cast when exposed.

The Nature Center has three trails:

TIME STUDY TRAIL (Blue Trail)—The theme of this trail is that everything changes; nothing is permanent. It begins in a 30-year-old pine forest and travels up a drumlin formed 11,000 years ago. Erosion, tree growth rings, and weathering are examples of factors visible from this trail.

FORESTRY TRAIL (Green Trail)—This is a forest management trail that winds through a mixed pine plantation. Examples of pruning, thinning methods, and timber cruising are provided along this trail.

WILDLIFE TRAIL (Orange Trail)—Wildlife management techniques are emphasized along this trail, including control of aquatic plants, field border plantings, fish stocking, shrub plantings, and strip mowing. It begins in a marsh, travels by a pond, and continues through a hardwood stand to an open field.

31) Sodus Bay Lighthouse Museum

The Sodus Bay Lighthouse Museum is operated by the Sodus Bay Historical Society of 7606 N. Ontario Street, Sodus Point. The nonprofit institution, which was chartered by the State in 1979, is supported by contributions and memberships.

The Sodus Bay region has been known for its commercial fishing, ice industry, grain exports, lumber trade, and shipbuilding. The first settlers entered the area in the late 1700s, and Sodus Bay became a busy harbor for exporting farm products and other commodities. Congress appropriated $4,500 for the construction of a lighthouse and keeper's house on the site in 1824; Ishmael Hill was the first lighthouse keeper.

Congress appropriated $14,000 in 1869 to replace the original structures, which had deteriorated beyond mere maintenance. That lighthouse was used from 1871 until 1901. The west pier, constructed in 1834 at the new entrance to the bay, was a more favorable location for the beacon and light that were installed in 1901. The lighthouse on the west pier was used as a residence for maintenance personnel until 1984.

The lighthouse served an area with heavy traffic of both commercial and pleasure boats. A railroad connecting Sodus Point with the coal fields of Pennsylvania was completed in 1872, along with a small coal loading trestle at the west end of the bay. The trestle was expanded considerably in 1927; in the five-year period 1861-1865, seven and a half million tons of coal were shipped using the trestle. While the wooden trestle was being dismantled in 1971, it caught fire and was destroyed.

Sodus Bay Lighthouse Museum, Sodus Point

The area served by the lighthouse, which has been a popular summertime recreation spot since the 1850s, is used by boaters, campers, fisherman, and picnickers. Sunday afternoon concerts are held on the grounds from Fourth of July weekend through Labor Day weekend. It is also a center for winter activities such as ice boating, ice fishing, and snowmobiling. The Sodus Bay Lighthouse Museum, which is open from May 1 through October 31, Tuesday through Sunday, contains many nautical artifacts and items of local history. Its D. Russell Chamberlain Memorial Library is open during museum hours. The museum is also open by appointment for adult group tours, bus tours, and school group tours.

32) Wayne County Historical Society Museum

The Wayne County Historical Society Museum, at 21 Butternut Street in Lyons, is located in a brick Italianate house and an attached stone building that served as the sheriff's residence and county jail for 107 years. The museum has exhibits on Erie Canal times, the early glass and pottery industries, Indian life, pre-historic times, and Wayne County military history.

Visitors can enter a replica of a general store in the circa 1910 barn located behind the museum. The museum also displays a collection of diverse transportation artifacts, including an 1860 coach and the only known surviving wooden canal horse bridge. The second floor contains exhibits of the rural history of Wayne County, including displays of carpentry, coopering, farming, ice harvesting, and lumbering.

33) Chimney Bluffs State Park

Chimney Bluffs State Park, an undeveloped state park known as a "natural park," is accessible off East Bay Road, two and a half miles east of Sodus Point. The natural park, which consists of pinnacles and spires that have been carved out by hundreds of years of water and wind erosion, extends along the Lake Ontario shoreline for over a mile.

The park can be viewed from a hiking trail inland from the bluffs, and from a narrow strip of beach between the bluffs and Lake Ontario. Since the chimney bluffs can be easily damaged by foot and vehicle traffic, hiking on the bluff faces and off-road vehicle use are prohibited.

34) Galen Marsh State Wildlife Management Area

The Galen Wildlife Management Area, located two miles southwest of the village of Clyde, consists of two parcels. The 562 acres in the larger parcel is accessible by River Road; the smaller parcel of 179 acres on Creager Island can be reached by boat or canoe from either the Clyde River or the Erie Canal. The Galen Wildlife Management Area has extensive frontage on the Erie Canal.

The Management Area consists of agricultural fields, marshes, upland woodlots, and wooded flood plains. It provides a habitat for deer, ducks, geese, great blue herons, songbirds, raccoons, and woodpeckers. Hunting, trapping, and fishing for bass, bullhead, and walleye pike are popular activities.

The Galen Wildlife Management Area was purchased in 1980 with funds from the Wetland Preservation Category of the 1972 Environmental Quality Bond Act. It provides protection for a portion of the Galen Marsh, known locally as the Marengo Swamp. Camping, off-road vehicle use, motorized boating, snowmobiling, and swimming are prohibited in the Wildlife Management Area. Permitted activities are:

- Bird-watching
- Canoeing
- Cross-country skiing
- Fishing
- Hiking
- Hunting
- Nature study
- Picnicking
- Trapping

THINGS TO DO

35) Alasa Farms

Alasa Farms, located at 6450 Shaker Road in Alton, is a contraction of the names of two former owners, Alvah Strong and Asa McBride. It is currently a 700-acre working farm that includes twelve acres of barns, buildings and dwellings. The central area is surrounded by pastureland, woods, 65 acres of orchards, and 200 acres of tillable crop land.

The farm tour includes a visit to the horse barn that used to house the hackney ponies. Varnished wainscoting is part of the interior woodwork of this magnificent barn. Grazing horses, sheep, and goats can be seen during a stroll around the fifteen acres of pasture on the farm. Children have the opportunity to feed and pet some of the animals in a petting corral behind the barn.

The Alasa Farm Museum is located in the only remaining large Shaker barn on the property, which was constructed over 150 years ago from timber harvested from surrounding forests. The barn contains a corn crib, livestock quarters, and a hog scalding cauldron used by the Shakers. The museum houses artifacts from an archaeological dig on the farm and a display of farming equipment.

For an additional fee, visitors can tour the Main Dwelling House, which is a private residence. The home contains some original window glass and Shaker pegboard and staircases. The third floor has been renovated in the Shaker tradition with authentic Shaker furniture.

The Shaker Heritage Antique Show is held annually on Alasa Farms in July. It features many out-of-state dealers offering Shaker originals as well as reproductions and fine Americana.

36) Sodus Shaker Festival

One day every other summer, Alasa Farms returns to its heritage as a Shaker Community, a nineteenth-century utopian society. Alasa Farms hosts the Sodus Shaker Festival in July in even-numbered years.

Members of the United Society of Believers in Christ's Second Coming were known as Shakers, because of the shaking and quivering dances they performed during religious services. They bought the tract of 1,400 acres in 1826 and built the Shaker Dwelling House in 1834. The house, which was inhabited by sixty people, had an ice-house wing on the east side. The cluster of simple white buildings is located on a ridge overlooking Sodus Bay, south of Sodus Point and east of the hamlet of Alton.

The Shakers lived simply; they were known for the simplicity of the design of everything they built, from early washing machines to dressers, ladder-back chairs, and tables. They sold baskets, brooms, brushes, and furniture, and are credited with being the first to market seeds in packets commercially.

In 1836, the Sodus Shaker Community moved to Groveland, south of Mt. Morris. Until 1892, 150 Shakers lived on 1,800 acres of rich Groveland farmland containing over thirty buildings, including barns, homes, mills, and a church. Their community was sold in 1893 to the Craig Colony for Epileptics. It became the Livingston County Correctional Facility.

Sodus Shaker Festivals features Shaker authorities on various aspects of Shaker life, craftsmen demonstrating Shaker crafts and selling Shaker reproductions, and Shaker music and dances.

37) Liberty Erie Canal Cruises

Cruises are provided on the 49-passenger *Liberty* from Village Park in Lyons. Several cruises are offered:

- a "coffee and danish" cruise lasting an hour and a half
- a buffet lunch cruise
- excursions to Creagger's Island, Newark, or Port Gibson, of two to four hours duration
- a buffet dinner and evening cruise
- a narrated canal study trip covering Ganargua Creek, Clinton's Ditch, Erie Canal, Barge Canal, and the dry dock in Lyons.

Almost all public cruises pass through a canal lock, either at Lyons or Newark. The *Liberty* is available for charter cruises.

SOUTH OF THE CANAL

PLACES TO SEE

Between Geneva and the Canal

38) Amberg Wine Cellars

Amberg Wine Cellars, at 2412 Seneca Castle Road, northwest of Geneva, was established in 1990. It is run by the Amberg family, who have been grape growers in the Seneca Lake area for decades. They have supplied root stock to area growers for over thirty years as Amberg's Grafted Grape Vine Nursery. The winery is located in the old barns of a farm that was established in 1795. Seneca Castle Road is approximately four miles west of Geneva, off Routes 5 and 20; the winery is near the intersection of Seneca Castle Road and County Road 23. The winery also has a retail store west of Geneva on Routes 5 and 20.

The winery produces both varietal wines and blends. Their vineyards are planted with Chardonnay, Pinot Noir, Riesling, Chambourcin (a French-American hybrid red), and Traminette and Vidal Blanc (hybrid white) vines. Amberg Wine Cellars currently produces more than 5,000 gallons annually of Chardonnay, Riesling, Pinot Noir, and their blends, including Blanc, Burgundy, and Pearl. The winery also offers a blush wine and Gypsy, which is a blend of Traminette and Riesling.

Winemaker Eric Amberg acquired his winemaking expertise at wineries in California, Germany, and New York State after earning his degree in enology at Fresno State in California.

39) Hoffman Clock Museum

The Hoffman Clock Museum, which is located in the Newark Public Library at the corner of Mason and High Streets in Newark, has over 100 horological items on display—mainly nineteenth-century American clocks. The collection has fifteen clocks made in New York State, and includes Dutch, English, French, German, and early Japanese clocks as well. Their collection includes a 1760 enameled watch, an 1815 banjo clock, and an 1875 oriental clock.

The museum's exhibits provide an opportunity to learn about the history of timekeeping. They introduce visitors to the development of timekeeping technology and clock styles. The unique collection of timepieces has something for everyone—young and old, novice and expert. Each travel season, a particular facet of timekeeping is highlighted in a special display.

The core collection was assembled by Augustus and Jennie Hoffman of Newark. The Hoffman Foundation, established in 1950, was organized to preserve the Hoffmans' collection for the education and enjoyment of the community. The museum is open daily during regular library hours, Monday through Saturday. However, the library and the museum are closed Saturdays during July and August. Arrangements for group tours of the museum may be made with the curator. Admission to the museum is free.

Geneva

40) Seneca Lake State Park

Seneca Lake State Park is located on 141 acres on Routes 5 and 20, one mile east of Geneva, along the northern end of Seneca Lake. The City of Geneva reclaimed an area of brush, marsh, and trees, and developed a city park on the site in 1922. In 1935, bones, projectile points, and tool artifacts were found, which archaelogists determined were from a pre-Iroquois Lamoka culture that existed about 4,000 years ago. Geneva transferred the city park lands to the State of New York in 1957 to develop Seneca Lake State Park, which was established in 1962.

The park has electrical hookups, pavillions, picnic areas with tables and fireplaces, playgrounds, playing fields, pay telephones, hot showers, and flush toilets. There are 200 seasonal boat slips, twenty transient boat slips, a boat launching site, and marine sewage pumpout facilities. Swimming is restricted to the designated lifeguard area. The season is from April 1 through October 23.

41) Hobart / William Smith Colleges

Hobart College is an independent liberal arts college for men and William Smith College is an independent liberal arts college for women; the two colleges form a coordinate system. Students of the two colleges take all classes together and are taught by a single faculty, but have separate student governments, athletic programs, and administrative support. Hobart College, founded in 1822, has 1,000 students, and William Smith College, founded in 1908, has 800 students.

The 170-acre campus, which borders Seneca Lake in Geneva, has twenty-eight classroom and administrative buildings, forty-seven residence halls, and a 105-acre nature preserve and outdoor laboratory located nearby. Ninety-six percent of the faculty hold doctoral degrees; the faculty to student ratio is approximately thirteen to one.

Both colleges are accredited by the Middle States Association of Colleges and Secondary Schools. In sports, Hobart College is known particularly for its lacrosse team, which has won the NCAA Division III lacrosse title on many occasions and now plays in Division I; William Smith College consistently ranks in the top ten in women's soccer.

42) Prouty-Chew Museum

Prouty-Chew Museum, owned and administered by the Geneva Historical Society, is located at 543 South Main Street, Geneva, at the intersection of Routes 5 and 20 and Route 14. The house also serves as the Geneva Historical Society's main offices. The Prouty-Chew House was built in 1829 by Charles Butler, a Geneva attorney, as a Federal-style home.

The home was changed and enlarged by the Prouty family in the 1850s and 1870s. In 1969, the Chew family conveyed the house to the Geneva Historical Society, who restored it and furnished it in the two major architectural styles it represents, Federal and Victorian.

Changing exhibitions are offered throughout the year: art exhibits, costume exhibits of selections from the Museum's costume collection, and exhibits related to local history. The Museum has a permanent exhibition called "Early Geneva, 1700-1830: the Development of Geneva through photos, text, graphics, and artifacts." The Museum also offers special events, such as the Annual Antique Show and Sale at Rose Hill Mansion, a Christmas Open House, and a Fall and Spring Lecture Series.

43) Rose Hill Mansion

Rose Hill, an 1839 Greek Revival mansion, is located east of Geneva, one mile south of Routes 5 and 20 on Route 96A. The mansion, owned and administered by the Geneva Historical Society, was declared a National Historic Landmark in 1988 by the National Park Service, for "possessing national significance in commemorating the history of the United States."

Rose Hill is one of the country's finest examples of Greek-Revival architecture. Six two-story Ionic columns support the central portico, and a cupola caps the central part of the mansion. The central section has symmetrical wings, with one-story Ionic columns.

Guided tours are conducted through twenty rooms decorated with wood and plaster moldings and furnished in the Empire style popular during the Greek-Revival period. The paint colors, draperies, and wallpaper used in the restoration of the mansion are typical of the period, as is the wall-to-wall carpeting. Most of the furniture is made of mahogany, a popular wood of the time. The high-ceilinged rooms, with their large windows and hefty doors, are hung with the paintings of former owners, including a painting by Severin Rosen of Williamsport, Pennsylvania.

The French crystal chandelier in the huge banquet hall is one of a pair made about 1810. Its mate hangs in Lemon Hill, a restored mansion in Fairmont Park, Philadelphia. The stairway's mahogany railing curves upward for three floors, capped by a skylight.

The Jenny Lynd bedroom contains the original Jenny Lynd bed. The "Swedish Nightingale" was brought to the United States in 1850 by impresario and showman P. T. Barnum. A London Theatre manager told Jenny that Barnum was a cheap showman

Rose Hill Mansion, Geneva

with no friends of culture. To dispel the rumor, Barnum asked his friends, the Shelton family, to entertain Jenny at their home, Greystone, in Derby, Connecticut. The bed in the Jenny Lynd bedroom at Rose Hill is the bed in which Miss Lynd slept at Greystone; it was widely copied by cabinetmakers in a line of "Jenny Lynd" furniture.

An early owner of the Rose Hill estate was Dr. Alexander Coventry, who bought the land in 1792, and named the property Fairhill after his ancestral home in Scotland. He built his house, not on the high ground on which Rose Hill stands, but near the lake shore, adjacent to the marshes of the Seneca River. Dr. Coventry, considering the property to be unhealthy, sold the 900-acre Fairhill farm to Robert Selden Rose, a Virginia planter and lawyer, in the early 1800s. Rose built a plain house on the site of the present mansion in 1809, which was later moved a short distance north to become the present carriage house. The kitchen of the original Rose house, with its brick fireplace and beehive oven in the hearth, became part of Rose Hill Mansion.

Rose was elected to the State Assembly in 1811, 1820, and 1821 and was a member of Congress from 1823 to 1827. He was a principal of the Seneca Lock Navigation Company formed to improve navigation between Seneca and Cayuga Lakes, a trustee of Hobart College, and the first vice president of New York State Agricultural Society upon its founding in 1832. He died in 1835, and the farm was sold to General William K. Strong, a retired wool merchant from New York City. Strong built the mansion on Rose's hill in 1839. One of General Strong's guests at Rose Hill was President Martin Van Buren. Upon the death of his wife, Sarah Van Giesen of Geneva, Strong returned to New York City to become vice president of the Bank of North America.

The farm reached its peak under the next owner, Robert J. Swan, who received the mansion and 360 acres of the property in 1850 as a wedding gift from his father, a New York City merchant. Swan, who decided that he was more suited to agriculture than to his father's mercantile business, moved to the area to study farming with John Johnson, a neighbor of Rose Hill. Swan married Johnson's daughter, Margaret, and they began their forty-year residency at the mansion in 1850.

Swan, who turned Rose Hill into one of the most productive farms in the state, won the three silver cups on display in the carriage house for his agricultural ability. He was awarded first prize for a premium farm in 1853 by the New York State Agricultural Society for comprehensive experiments in the use of drainage tiles to drain marshy land. He installed the first large-scale tile drainage system in the early 1850s.

He received another award in 1858, and he was one of the first to use the reaper successfully on his principal crop, wheat. He was one of the incorporators of the State College of Agriculture in 1853, and he played a significant role in establishing the New York State Agricultural Experiment Station in Geneva.

By 1965, Rose Hill had become run down and the mansion, with two and a half acres of land, went on the market for $15,000. Swan's grandson, Waldo Hutchins, Jr., purchased it, along with fifteen acres in front to protect its view of the lake and five acres in the rear, as a gift to the Geneva Historical Society. The historical society restored the mansion to its 1840s condition, and it was opened to the public on September 28, 1968. Hutchins dedicated the mansion to his mother, Agnes Swan Hutchins, who was born and grew to adulthood at Rose Hill.

Rose Hill Mansion is open from May through October on Monday through Saturday and on Sunday afternoons. A nominal admission fee is charged.

44) Mike Weaver Drain Tile Museum

The Mike Weaver Drain Tile Museum, on East Lake Road just south of Rose Hill Mansion, is located in the restored home of John and Margaret Johnson. John Johnson introduced tile drainage to America in 1835. The museum houses a collection of over 350 different styles of tiles dating from 100 BC until the present time.

The museum has an orientation room on tiling and a research room containing many original documents and written material on tiling. The Johnsons' living room is furnished with many pieces of the original furniture. The museum is open from May 1 to October 31 by appointment only. Call or visit Rose Hill Mansion for admission.

THINGS TO DO

Between Geneva and the Canal

45) Sauerkraut Festival

Phelps, the home of the annual Sauerkraut Festival since 1967, has been a center for cabbage growing and sauerkraut factories for much of its history. The annual Sauerkraut Festival is held at the Phelps firemen's field on Ontario Street in early August. The festival provides music, parades, and food, including plenty of sauerkraut.

Previous years' festivals have included an early evening children's parade, children's night on the midway, and a DJ on Thursday. Friday's activities are midway rides, a block dance at the American Legion on Main Street with music of the 1950s, 1960s, and 1970s, and live music at the festival grounds. Saturday's activities have included:

- Arts and crafts
- Midway rides
- Festival parade
- Chicken and pork barbecues
- Cutting of the sauerkraut cake
- Continuous live music
- A 20K race over country roads from Phelps to Clifton Springs and back
- Special music events, such as bagpipers and cloggers
- A bike rodeo
- Fireworks

Events scheduled for Sunday are arts and crafts, bike tours, a custom car show, a chicken barbecue at the American Legion, live music, and midway rides.

Geneva

46) The Smith Opera House

The Smith Opera House, 82 Seneca Street, Geneva, is both a movie theatre and a theatre for the performing arts. Its thirty-by forty-foot movie screen is the largest in central New York. The opera house is one of only twenty-one "Great American Movie Palaces" left in New York, of which only five are still used as performing arts facilities. One of the five is Radio City Music Hall in New York City. Only about 300 of the more than 3,000 theatres of this type in the United States still exist. The Smith Opera House was almost destroyed in 1981 to provide space for a parking lot but was saved by the Finger Lakes Regional Arts Council.

Due to the modifications that it underwent over the years, its architecture is an eclectic mixture of Art Deco, Spanish baroque, and Victorian styles. The theatre's original facade was "Richardsonian," with a terra cotta arch carved with the likenesses of Edwin Booth and William Shakespeare. The walls on the sides of the stage have golden cartouches with busts of Beethoven and Moliere. The theatre has excellent acoustics, and an unobstructed view of the stage is provided from all seats.

Geneva philanthropist William Smith paid $39,000 in 1894 to fulfill his dream of an opera house for the city. It opened on October 29, 1894, with James O'Neill, the father of playwright Eugene O'Neill, starring in the play *The Count of Monte Cristo*. Other famous entertainers who have performed at the opera house are Sarah Bernhardt, George M. Cohan, Tommy Dorsey, Isadora Duncan, Arthur Fiedler, Al Jolson, John Philip Sousa, and Ellen Terry.

The Smith Opera House was used as a vaudeville house / playhouse until the early 1900s, when it was donated to Hobart College. Hobart sold it to help endow William Smith College at its founding in 1908. Schine Enterprises bought the building in 1929 and totally renovated it as the flagship of the Schine chain of theatres. Architect Victor Rigaumount designed a ceiling of stars in an evening sky, utilized Art Deco-style signs and trim, and chose Victorian-style light fixtures.

Performances at the Smith Opera House in recent years have

included the "Acrobats" from the Peoples' Republic of China, Berkshire Ballet's *Nutcracker*, "Blood, Sweat, and Tears," the Rochester Philharmonic Orchestra, Bruce Springsteen, the Syracuse Symphony Orchestra conducted by Mitch Miller, and the U.S. Air Force Band of the East. The Smith Opera House is the home of the Finger Lakes Symphony Orchestra and the Geneva Theatre Guild.

47) Boat Rides on the Seneca Dreamer

The Seneca Boat Company operates the *Seneca Dreamer,* a 149-passenger paddle-wheeler tour and dining boat from Lakeshore Park, Geneva. The Seneca Boat Company provides scenic narrated cruises, dinner cruises, sunset cruises, and moonlight cruises from May to October.

48) Belhurst Castle— Historic Restaurant and Inn

Belhurst Castle, an inn and restaurant constructed of red Medina stone, is located on Route 14, just south of the Geneva city line. The Castle, with its twenty-five acres of sweeping lawn, gardens, and over-100-year-old maples, oaks, and pines overlooking the west shore of Seneca Lake, has been a home, a speak-easy, a casino, and a restaurant. Belhurst ("beautiful forest") Castle was constructed from 1885 to 1889 in Richardson-Romanesque style, mainly of materials imported from Europe.

In 1885, Carrie Harron Collins, a newly married Cincinnati society figure and a descendant of Henry Clay, commissioned architect Albert W. Fuller to design the castle home in which she and her husband lived for forty years. Fuller designed it with turrets, a covered carriage entrance, a third-floor Victorian dancing room, and carved wood paneling for both its private and public rooms.

After the death of Mrs. Collins in 1926, Belhurst Castle was purchased by a local gambler, Cornelius "Red" Dwyer. The flamboyant Dwyer was born in Lyons, New York, worked as a fireman on the railroad, and moved in the milieu of plush gambling halls across the state during prohibition. He operated the castle as a speak-easy, with a gambling casino on the second floor. Many well-known performers, including Sophie Tucker, entertained guests during those years. The upstairs gaming rooms were closed in the early 1950s when Dwyer was summoned to hearings in Washington conducted by Senator Estes Kefauver.

Part of the Belhurst Castle is now operated as an inn with thirteen rooms, including two two-room suites. Mrs. Collins' bedroom, with its amber glass panes, extends the length of the large living room. The bedroom contains an ornately carved 1810 mahogany four-poster bed so high that a bedside stool is required to climb into it. At the other end of the living room is Room 3, with a couch and three armchairs clustered around a marble fireplace, and a dining table in the circular alcove of the turret.

The dancing room on the third floor, with an eighteen-foot ceiling and closed-in porch, has been converted to a suite with a spacious sauna. With its lookout in the turret's attic, this suite is the most expensive accommodation in the Inn. The spacious guest rooms, all with modern baths, are furnished with valuable antiques and oriental rugs, and most of them have working fireplaces.

Dinner is accompanied by piano music. As a pleasant after-dinner pastime, guests can sit in the ornate parlor, with its carved white Honduran mahogany moldings, quarter-cut cherry mantelpieces, and white oak banisters, and listen to the music. Or they may walk across the lawn, sit on the park benches overlooking Seneca Lake, and watch the boats go by. While relaxing, one can speculate on a tale in the brochure that describes Belhurst Castle:

> Tales persist of the romantic past that began before the present structure was built—of the doomed romance of the runaway Spanish Don and his beautiful Italian opera singer lady love who once lived here, of secret tunnels and hidden treasures buried in the walls or on the grounds, of ghosts and hauntings, Fact or fancy? No one knows.

49) Geneva-on-the-Lake Resort

Geneva-on-the-Lake is a European-style vacation resort on the west shore of Seneca Lake at 1001 Lochland Road, on Route 14, south of Geneva's old-world historic district. The white Italianate villa, which has been nominated for the National Registry of Historic Places, is a copy of the Lancellotti Villa in Frascati, Italy. It is located on ten acres with a formal, hedged garden, a seventy-foot swimming pool, tall pines, and a path through woods to the lakeshore. The garden is bordered by Greek and Roman statues of Venus, Hermes, and Venus de Milo; the swimming pool is surrounded by columns topped with clay jardinieres in the style of a Borghese garden.

Geneva-on-the-Lake has twenty-nine suites, nineteen with one bedroom and ten with two bedrooms. Each suite has a living room, kitchen, and a full bath or a bath and a half.

The Classic suite is a two-bedroom suite with a canopied bed, two fireplaces, and a balcony overlooking the gardens and the lake. The Library suite is the original library of the Nester family, with a coffered ceiling, a four-poster bed, and a fireplace.

Landmark / Townhouse suites have one or two bedrooms. Some Landmark suites have historic architectural features. Townhouse suites have two bedrooms and a private terrace. Deluxe suites have one bedroom except for one studio with a fireplace and a balcony. Studio suites have a combination living room / bedroom with a queen-size fold-down bed. Geneva-on-the-Lake is furnished with period reproductions from the Stickley Furniture Company.

The villa was built in 1912 by the Nester family as a private residence. The Capuchin Monks bought the villa from the Nesters, and between 1949 and the early 1970s used it as a monastery. The Schickel family of Ithaca and Ohio purchased the resort and authorized a $2,000,000 renovation. Initially, they planned to operate it as an apartment complex, but, shortly after its completion, they decided to operate it as a resort.

Geneva-on-the-Lake has a dock, boathouse, moorings, and sailing facilities; guests may bring their own boat or rent one. The resort has conference facilities for executive meetings of up to thirty-five people, with three conference rooms. Geneva-on-the-Lake has a four-diamond rating from the American Automobile Association. Also, it is a member of the Organization of Distinguished Inns and Historic Hotels.

◆ ◆ ◆

Geneva-on-the-Lake Resort

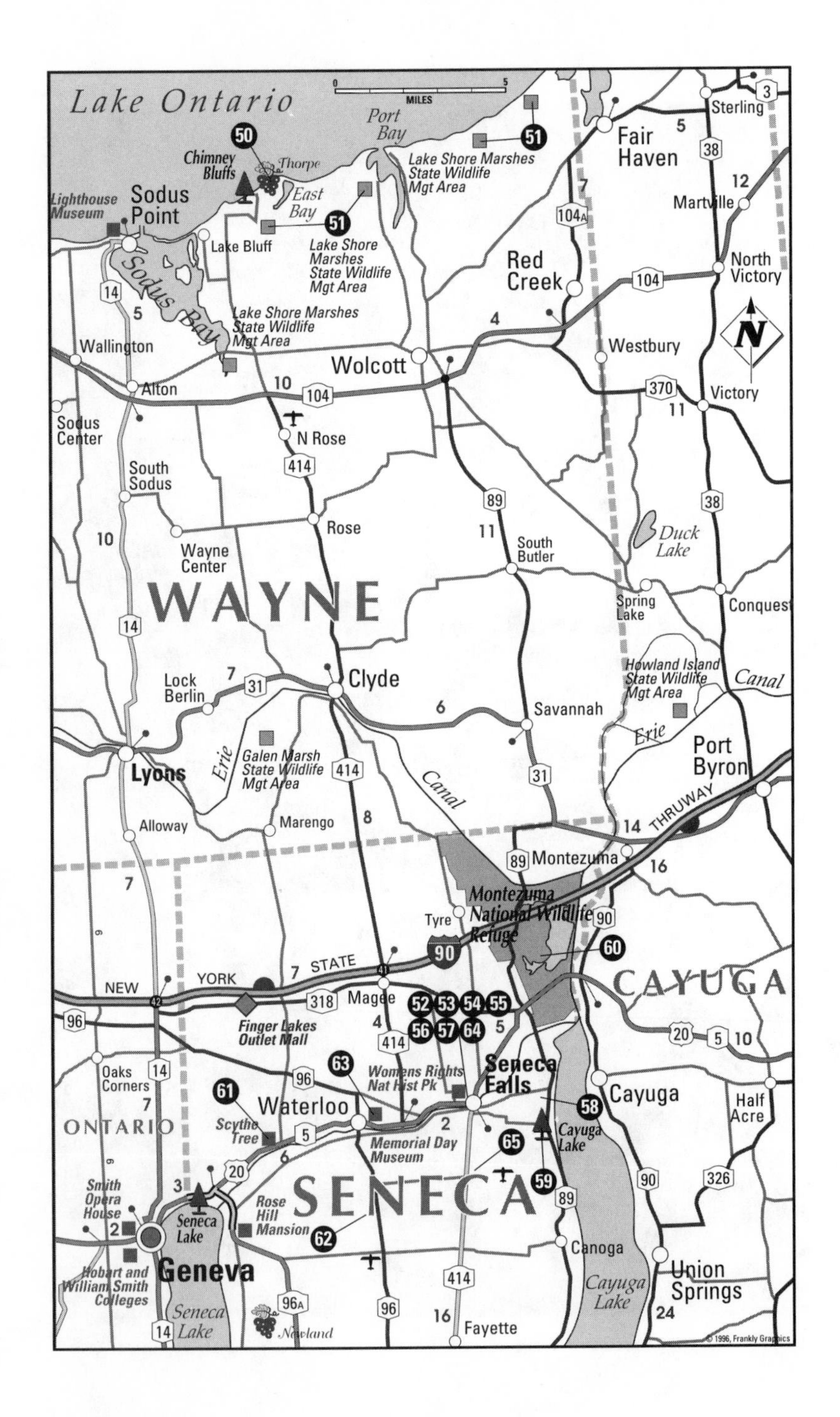

Lake Ontario
MILES
Port Bay
Chimney Bluffs
Thorpe
East Bay
Lake Shore Marshes State Wildlife Mgt Area
Lighthouse Museum
Sodus Point
Lake Bluff
Sodus Bay
Fair Haven
Sterling
Martville
Red Creek
North Victory
Wallington
Alton
Wolcott
Westbury
Victory
Sodus Center
N Rose
South Sodus
Rose
South Butler
Duck Lake
Wayne Center
WAYNE
Spring Lake
Conquest
Howland Island State Wildlife Mgt Area
Canal
Lock Berlin
Clyde
Savannah
Erie
Port Byron
Lyons
Galen Marsh State Wildlife Mgt Area
Canal
Alloway
Marengo
THRUWAY
Montezuma
Montezuma National Wildlife Refuge
Tyre
NEW YORK STATE
CAYUGA
Magee
Finger Lakes Outlet Mall
Oaks Corners
Womens Rights Nat Hist Pk
Seneca Falls
Cayuga
Half Acre
Waterloo
ONTARIO
Scythe Tree
Memorial Day Museum
Cayuga Lake
Smith Opera House
Seneca Lake
Rose Hill Mansion
SENECA
Canoga
Geneva
Hobart and William Smith Colleges
Cayuga Lake
Union Springs
Seneca Lake
Newland
Fayette
© 1996, Frankly Graphics

• *chapter six* •

From Seneca Falls / Waterloo to Lake Ontario

We were forty miles from Albany,
Forget it I never shall;
What a terrible storm we had one night
On the E-ri-e Canal.

Oh the E-ri-e was a-rising,
The gin was getting low;
And I scarcely think we'll get a drink
'Til we get to Buffalo.

We were loaded down with barley,
We were chuck up full of rye;
And the captain he looked down at me
With his [terrible] wicked eye.

Oh the girls are in the *Police Gazette*,
The crew are all in jail;
I'm the only sea-cook's son
That's left to tell the tale.

From *American Songbag* by Carl Sandburg

Seneca Falls—Brief Description and History

Seneca Falls is known as the Birthplace of Women's Rights in the United States. The first Women's Rights Convention was held there in 1848, when Elizabeth Cady Stanton, of Seneca Falls, presented her *Declaration of Sentiments* modeled on the *Declaration of Independence*, written by Thomas Jefferson. The convention was called by Ms. Stanton and her mentor, Lucretia Mott, a visiting Quaker from Philadelphia, and three other area women. Elizabeth Cady Stanton became the policymaker and spokeswoman for the Women's Rights Movement.

The first Women's Rights Convention was held in the Wesleyan Chapel. The chapel subsequently became Johnson's Opera House, a Ford dealership, and then a laundromat. The east and west walls and the roof have been restored.

The Women's Rights National Historic Park, dedicated in 1982, maintains a visitor center at 136 Fall Street and the 1832 Stanton home at 32 Washington Street. The National Women's Hall of Fame is located at 76 Fall Street. It was established in 1969 to "provide a permanent place of honor for America's most outstanding women, a place for people to visit and learn about the significant contributions—often against tremendous odds—that these women have made to our country," according to a Hall of Fame brochure.

The home of Amelia Jenks Bloomer, for whom bloomers are named, is at 63 E. Bayard Street. She wrote about the bloomer costume worn by members of the Women's Rights Movement in her temperance newspaper, *The Lily*, but she didn't invent bloomers. She published a picture of them that was widely copied.

Elizabeth Smith Miller, daughter of abolitionist Gerritt Smith, wore the costume, consisting of Turkish trousers and short skirts, when visiting Elizabeth Cady Stanton in 1849. Ms. Miller had seen a similar costume worn by Swiss nurses. Bloomers provided women with considerably more freedom of movement than the traditional hoops, petticoat, and five yards of skirts, which required lifting the hem to walk up steps.

Waterfalls that no longer exist provided Seneca Falls with its name; the fifty-foot drop in elevation of the Seneca River is now accommodated by Locks 2 and 3 on the Cayuga-Seneca Canal. Lawrence Van Cleef, an early settler, first visited the region as a member of the General Sullivan Expedition during the Revolutionary War. Early in the life of the village, the Bayard Company, a monopolistic land syndicate, obtained the water rights to the Seneca River and set high fees for its use early in the life of the settlement.

Colonel Wilhelminus Mynderse was an early agent for the syndicate that owned a grist mill and a store at the falls. The syndicate's high rates hindered development of the settlement until the state took over the water rights in 1827 to build the Cayuga-Seneca Canal parallel to the river. Most of the mills were concentrated along the river and on the islands between the canal and the river.

In 1915, the present configuration of the Cayuga-Seneca Canal was completed by joining the canal and the river, replacing the falls with the two locks and submerging the industrial islands, thus creating Van Cleef Lake. Trinity Episcopal Church on the lake, built in 1885-86 in early Gothic style, is one of the most photographed scenes in New York State. A park is also named for Van Cleef. The name Mynderse has also survived; the high school in Seneca Falls is called Mynderse Academy and the village library is Mynderse Library.

Wooden pumps were made in Seneca Falls beginning in 1840. In 1850, Seabury Gould began the manufacture of iron pumps at what is now the Gould Pump Company, a firm known worldwide for quality products.

The Montezuma Wildlife Refuge, maintained by the U.S. Fish and Wildlife Service of the Department of the Interior, is located a few miles north of Seneca Falls. Cayuga Lake State Park is located several miles southeast of the village, along the west shoreline of the lake.

Waterloo—Brief Description and History

Waterloo is west of and virtually contiguous with its neighbor, Seneca Falls. Waterloo is recognized as the birthplace of Memorial Day by the sanction of the U.S. Congress and by the presidential proclamation of President Lyndon Johnson in 1966. The village had the first community-wide observance of Memorial Day on May 5, 1866, when businesses closed and black-draped flags were flown at half-staff. Community leaders and veterans marched to three local cemeteries, where ceremonies were held and graves were decorated with evergreen boughs, floral crosses, and wreaths.

The Memorial Day Museum, a twenty-room brick mansion built in the 1830s, is located at 35 E. Main Street. The museum displays items pertinent to Memorial Day, the Civil War, World Wars I and II, and the Korean Conflict.

Credit for the origination of Memorial Day is sometimes given to southern women who placed flowers on the graves of both Confederate and Union soldiers. However, this was an uncoordinated activity that was not done on one particular day. On May 5, 1868, General John A. Logan, Commander-in-Chief of the Grand Army of the Republic, designated May 30, 1868, as the day for decorating the graves of those who died for their country during the Civil War. Thus, May 30th became known as "Decoration Day." The name was changed to Memorial Day in 1882, but people continued to use both names.

The idea of setting aside a day as "Memorial Day" was originally conceived by Henry C. E. Wells, a Waterloo merchant, and was supported by General John B. Murray of Waterloo, County Clerk of Seneca County. Murray became known as the "father of Memorial Day." In fairness, the two men should be called "the fathers of Memorial Day."

The Scythe Tree is two miles west of Waterloo on Routes 5 and 20. It is a large Balm of Gilead tree, of the poplar family, in which three scythes were imbedded by Waterloo men leaving for war. The first scythe was placed in the tree by a Civil War soldier who didn't return from the war and the second two blades by two World War I military men who did return. This historical curiosity is marked by a nearby monument.

NORTH OF THE CANAL

PLACES TO SEE

50) Thorpe Vineyard and Farm Winery

The Thorpe Vineyard and Farm Winery, located at 8150 Chimney Heights Boulevard in Wolcott, produces four Chimney Heights brand wines: Cayuga White, Chardonnay, Estate Blanc, and Pinot Noir. The vineyard was planted in 1978 and the first harvest was in 1983. Four additional varieties have been planted: Marechal Foch, Melody, Pinot Gris, and Riesling. The winery has expanded from an annual production of 250 cases to over 1,000 cases.

51) Lake Shore Marshes Wildlife Management Area

The Lake Shore Marshes Wildlife Management Area is located between Sodus Bay and Fair Haven Beach State Park in northeastern Wayne County. It consists of several parcels bounded on the north by Lake Ontario, and it contains 6,179 acres of wetlands and adjacent uplands. The area provides a combination of bay-lake-marsh environments that offer habitats for fish, mammals, shorebirds, songbirds, and waterfowl such as black ducks, mallards, teal, and wood ducks.

Popular activities are fishing for largemouth and smallmouth bass, northern pike, and panfish; hunting for deer, pheasants, rabbits, squirrels, and woodcock; and trapping for mink and muskrats. Bird-watching is another popular pastime in the Wildlife Management Area. Developments include boat access sites and trails for fishermen, hikers, hunters, and naturalists. Also, small water impoundments and parking areas at scenic locations overlooking areas used by migrating waterfowl have been constructed in the Wildlife Management Area.

SOUTH OF THE CANAL

PLACES TO SEE

Seneca Falls

52) Elizabeth Cady Stanton House

Elizabeth Cady Stanton was one of the organizers of the first Women's Rights Convention on July 19 and 20, 1848, and was the author of the *Declaration of Sentiments* read at the convention. She became the major author, policymaker, and speechmaker for the Women's Rights Movement. Her friend, Susan B. Anthony, became the Movement's main organizer.

Elizabeth Cady and Henry Brewster Stanton were married on May 1, 1840, in a ceremony omitting the vow "to obey." She preferred being addressed as Mrs. Elizabeth Cady Stanton instead of Mrs. Henry Stanton; she said she didn't like being called Henry. In 1847, the Stantons moved from Boston to 32 Washington Street, Seneca Falls. They lived there with their seven children until 1862.

Commenting on the lack of intellectual and cultural pursuits she had enjoyed in Boston and feeling burdened with housework and child care, Elizabeth Cady Stanton wrote in her autobiography *Eighty Years and More*:

> The general discontent I felt with women's portion as wife, mother, housekeeper, physician, and spiritual guide, the chaotic conditions into which everything fell without my constant supervision, the wearied anxious look of the majority of women, impressed me with a strong feeling that some active measures should be taken to remedy the wrongs ... [done to] women....

The Elizabeth Cady Stanton House is owned by the National Park Service. The existing portion of the house has been restored to its 1848 appearance and is open to the public.

53) National Women's Hall of Fame

The National Women's Hall of Fame is located at 76 Fall Street, Seneca Falls. Its goal is "to honor in perpetuity those women, citizens of the United States of America, whose contribution to the arts, athletics, business, education, government, humanities, philanthropy and science, have been of the greatest value for the development of their country."

The permanent exhibits of the National Women's Hall of Fame focus on the lives of women inducted through public nomination. Each year two more women are nominated. At least seven of the Hall of Fame honorees have Finger Lakes ties: Susan B. Anthony, Rochester; Clara Barton, Dansville; Antoinette Brown Blackwell, Henrietta; Elizabeth Blackwell, Geneva; Margaret Sanger, Corning; Elizabeth Cady Stanton, Seneca Falls; and Harriet Tubman, Auburn. Other inductees include Jane Addams, Dorothea Dix, Helen Keller, Margaret Mead, Alice Paul, Eleanor Roosevelt, and Sojourner Truth.

In addition to permanent exhibits, changing exhibits to interpret women's role in society use portraits, photographs, letters, and memorabilia. Tours are available.

54) Women's Rights National Historic Park Visitor Center

The Women's Rights National Historic Park operates a visitor center at 136 Fall Street, Seneca Falls. A schedule of activities is posted in the center, which houses many exhibits. An orientation video and a 25-minute movie, "Dreams of Equality," are available for viewing.

Twenty bronze statues of organizers of the first Women's Rights Convention, men who supported the organizers, and convention attendees face visitors as they enter the Visitor Center. The statues are likenesses of Elizabeth Cady Stanton, Frederick Douglass, Martha Wright, Lucretia and James Mott, Mary Ann and Thomas McClintock, Jane and Richard Hunt, and eleven unidentified convention attendees.

Women's Rights National Historic Park Visitor Center, Seneca Falls

The second floor of the Visitor Center has displays of the *Declaration of Sentiments*, plus displays such as "Inauguration of a Rebellion," "True Womanhood," "School Matters," "Campaigning Women Fashioning an Image," and "Women at Work." The second floor also includes temporary exhibit space and a classroom.

The Visitor Center, which includes a bookstore, is open daily year-round except for Thanksgiving Day, Christmas Day, and New Year's Day. The center is fully accessible to the mobility impaired.

Declaration Park, which is adjacent to the Visitor Center, features a commemorative waterwall engraved with the words of the *Declaration of Sentiments* and the names of the 100 women who signed the document.

55) Wesleyan Chapel

The Wesleyan Chapel, adjacent to Women's Rights National Historic Park Visitor Center, was the site of the first Women's Rights Convention on July 19 and 20, 1848. The chapel subsequently became Johnson's Opera House, a Ford dealership, and a laundromat. The remains of the chapel, the roof and side walls, have been restored.

56) Urban Cultural Park—Village of Seneca Falls

The Village of Seneca Falls Urban Cultural Park operates a visitor center in the historic Partridge Building at 115 Fall Street. The visitor center is open daily on Monday through Saturday and on Sunday afternoons. The Urban Cultural Center focuses on the themes of industrialization, reform movements, and transportation. It highlights the village's role in the development of the Women's Rights Movement.

The village's history as a center of water-powered industry and transportation is depicted in exhibits and audiovisual programs. On display are locally manufactured goods, such as bells, pumps, and tools. Fiber optic maps illuminate the systems of canals, highways, railroads, and turnpikes that contributed to the development of industry and the spread of the ideas of social reform. The history of the mill owners is displayed, along with the contributions of the Irish and Italian men and women who built and operated the canals and factories.

57) Seneca Falls Historical Society Museum

The Victorian mansion at 55 Cayuga Street is the home of the Seneca Falls Historical Society. The twenty-three-room home was built in Italianate style in 1855 by Edward Mynderse, the son of an early settler. In 1880, Ellen Partridge bought the house and contracted the prominent Rochester architect, James D. Cutler, to enlarge and redesign the home in the popular Queen Anne style. Many of the furnishings and art pieces are from the Becker family, who lived in the house for over fifty years.

The mansion is decorated with the original chandeliers and light fixtures, intricately carved golden oak woodwork, ornate door hinges, carpet loomed in France, and mid-nineteenth-century wallpaper. The stained glass windows in the stairwell were designed by W. J. McPherson of Boston. A sunflower motif, which was the symbol of the Aesthetic Movement, is displayed in the doors, glass, and woodwork. In the butler's pantry and kitchen, visitors are reminded of the long-vanished era of the coal cook stove, ice box, and water pump.

A tea set used by President James Monroe during his administration is displayed in a special exhibit in the front parlor. Mary Lincoln purchased new china when she and President Lincoln moved into the White House. She gave the tea set in the exhibit to William Seward, who was Lincoln's Secretary of State. The tea set was later acquired by the Seneca Falls Historical Society. Both Eleanor Roosevelt and Jacqueline Kennedy asked for it to be returned to the White House, but the Historical Society voted to keep it on display.

The Museum's extensive archives, photographic collection, and library are used by researchers throughout the United States. The library and archives are open for scholarly and genealogical research; assistance is available. The collections are particularly rich in the areas of the Civil War, local history, and women's history. The Museum sponsors lectures, classes and workshops for children and activities during Convention Days and Empire State Farm Days. It is open from 9 a.m. to 5 p.m. on Mondays through Fridays, and from noon until 4 p.m. on Saturdays. During the summer, the Museum is open Sunday afternoons from noon until 4 p.m.

58) New York Chiropractic College

The New York Chiropractic College was located in Old Brookville, Long Island, until September, 1991, when it moved to the Eisenhower College Campus, outside Seneca Falls. The college has outpatient facilities in Levittown, Long Island, and Syracuse. Over 650 students attend the college.

59) Cayuga Lake State Park

Cayuga Lake State Park, established in 1928, is located three miles southeast of Seneca Falls, off Route 89, at 2678 Lower Lake Road. Oak-shaded lawns and sandy beach areas extend along the lake in this 141-acre park. The terrain is flat at the lakeshore, and slants slighty uphill toward the campgrounds; the lake off the swimming area is just over five feet deep. The park has a boat launching ramp; fishing is a popular activity.

The park has 286 campsites (250 non-electric, 36 electric, RVs allowed), fourteen cabins, flush toilets, hot showers, and a trailer dumping station. The park also has a bath house, a concession stand, a recreation building, and three pavilions, as well as playing fields, a playground, and picnic areas with tables and fireplaces. The park, which is accessible to the mobility impaired, is open all winter for cross-country skiing, hiking, ice fishing, sledding, and snowmobiling.

60) Montezuma National Wildlife Refuge

The Montezuma National Wildlife Refuge, established in 1937, is located at 3395 Routes 5 and 20, east of Seneca Falls. It is bounded by the New York State Barge Canal to the north, the

Cayuga Lake outlet to the barge canal to the east, and Cayuga Lake and the Cayuga-Seneca Canal to the south. The western boundary, comprised of Route 89, Lay Road, and Durling Road, is irregular.

The refuge is maintained by the U.S. Fish and Wildlife Service, Department of the Interior, primarily as a feeding, nesting, and resting habitat for migratory waterfowl. A total of 282 species of birds have been seen in the refuge, including Canada geese, herons, mallards, northern harriers (marsh hawks), osprey, rails, redwing blackbirds, shorebirds, snipe, songbirds, teal, terns, and wood ducks.

The largest concentrations of waterfowl can be seen during migration; 140,000 Canada geese have been observed in April and 150,000 ducks in October. The spring migration of waterfowl such as Canada geese has lessened in number in recent years. However, several hundred Canada geese maintain a year-round home at the refuge and can be seen making excursions to and from off-refuge feeding areas.

Muskrats, white-tailed deer, and woodchucks can also be observed in their habitats in the refuge. Muskrats are controlled to provide the necessary combination of open water and vegetation for food and cover for the waterfowl. Since muskrats use water plants to construct their houses and for food, too many muskrats deplete plant cover for the waterfowl and too few muskrats allow the plants to take over the open water.

The prime times for viewing wildlife are early in the morning and late in the day (the Refuge is open from sunrise to sunset). A three-and-a-half-mile auto tour route, two twenty-foot observation towers, and a two and one-fifth mile nature trail give ample opportunity for observing wildlife. Esker Brook Nature Trail, west of Route 89, is a mildly sloping loop that follows Esker Brook; it is an excellent location for finding songbirds.

The visitor center provides a diorama exhibit, leaflets, and a small information room, as well as rest rooms and public telephones. A two-level observation deck with a spotting telescope is available at the back of the visitor center on the second level. The observation deck overlooks the 2,700-acre Main Pool, one of two large pools and five small pools in the refuge. The water level in the Main Pool is maintained at about two and a half feet for most of its area, but a portion of it is one foot deep for the use of mallards, pintails, and teal.

The other large pool is the 1,340-acre Tschache (pronounced "shocky") Pool, named for Ottley "Buck" Tschache, a former assistant refuge manager. It contains a great blue heron rookery and is a bald eagle nesting and feeding area. By 1980, only one breeding pair of bald eagles nested in New York State. A program to build up the bald eagle population was started in 1976 at the Montezuma Refuge by releasing young birds into the wild. Montezuma's efforts have been crucial in increasing the State's eagle population.

The five small pools in the refuge are the East Pool, the West Pool, May's Point Pool (known for shorebirds in the spring and fall), the North Spring Pool, and the South Spring Pool. The East Pool, along the outlet from Cayuga Lake to the New York State Barge Canal, has a dam and locks at its southern end. The West Pool is part of the Cayuga-Seneca Canal, and the South Spring Pool has a scenic overlook.

Fish, including carp, brown bullhead, northern pike, and walleye, are abundant in the canals and rivers on the periphery of the refuge. Fishing and boating are not allowed in the refuge, but three public fishing sites and a boat launch nearby allow access to the New York State Barge Canal from Cayuga Lake and the Clyde River.

Prior to 1900, the Montezuma Marsh extended north for twelve miles from Cayuga Lake and was eight miles wide at its widest point. Its importance as a refuge for wildlife was not recognized, and much of it was drained to make arable farms. By 1911, there were only 100 acres left undrained. It was eventually purchased by the federal government and became part of the National Wildlife Refuge System in 1934. It was established as the Montezuma National Wildlife Refuge in 1937 and was gradually expanded to its current 6,432 acre size.

Waterloo

61) The Scythe Tree

In October 1861, twenty-six-year-old James Wyman Johnson attended a recruiting rally in Waterloo at which two Grand Army of the Republic recruiting officers and the Rev. Dr. Samuel Gridley, pastor of the local Presbyterian church, spoke to gain recruits for President Lincoln's army. Wyman Johnson, waking early the morning after the rally, wrestled with the decision of whether to volunteer or to stay and help his parents run the farm. He went to the barn, took his scythe off its hook, and began to cut a field of tall grass, while mulling over his decision. Finally, he decided that it was his duty as the oldest son to volunteer. His brother and two sisters could help his father and mother run the farm.

He told his parents of his decision, placed his scythe in the crotch of a Balm of Gilead sapling (a tree of the poplar family), said "Leave this scythe in the tree until I return," and walked to Waterloo to join Company G of the 85th New York Volunteers. He fought in the battle of Fair Oaks, was captured in a battle at New Berne, North Carolina, and was released in an exchange of prisoners. At Plymouth, near Albemarle Sound, he was wounded in the thigh and taken to the Confederate Hospital at Raleigh, where he died of his wounds.

Wyman Johnson's parents refused to believe that their son was dead and hoped that he would return to take his scythe from the Balm of Gilead tree. In 1916, the grave of Wyman Johnson was found in a Confederate cemetery in Raleigh. His remains were moved to the National Cemetery in Arlington, Virginia. That same year, the Scythe Tree was struck by lightning, but neither the tree nor the scythe blade suffered any damage. The wooden handle of the scythe had long since rotted away.

In 1918, Scythe Tree Farm was owned by the C. L. Schaffer family. Both sons of the family, Raymond and Lynn, volunteered for service in World War I. Raymond joined Company F, 33rd Engineers, and his brother enlisted in the U. S. Navy. They both placed their scythes in the crotch of the Balm of Gilead tree before they left for training camp. Raymond and Lynn returned home safely from the war and removed the handles from their scythes in the tree, but left the blades in place, several feet above Wyman Johnson's blade.

Scythe Tree Farm is located two and a half miles west of Waterloo at 841 Waterloo-Geneva Road (Routes 5 and 20). The owners have always allowed public access to the tree. All three scythe blades can be seen extending from the tree, but less than six inches of the blade placed there in 1861 are visible.

62) Peter Whitmer Home

On April 6, 1830, at the home of Peter Whitmer, Joseph Smith, the first President of the Church of Jesus Christ of Latter-day Saints (Mormons), and five witnesses, formally signed the papers to organize the restored Church of Jesus Christ. The five witnesses were Oliver Cowdery, Joseph's brothers Hyrum and Samuel H. Smith, and Peter Whitmer and his brother, David. The home is a small, open-hearthed farm home in Fayette, two miles south of Waterloo, off Route 96. The visitor center is maintained by the Church of Jesus Christ of Latter-day Saints.

63) Memorial Day Museum

The Memorial Day Museum is located at 35 E. Main Street, Waterloo. The museum was built as a home in the 1830s and was extensively renovated in the 1860s, when two large wings were added. Eight large rooms of the twenty-room brick mansion are open to the public.

Waterloo was the site of the first Memorial Day celebration in May 1866 to honor local soldiers who died in the Civil War. The museum displays items pertinent to Memorial Day, the Civil War, World Wars I and II, and the Korean Conflict. The museum is open afternoons, Tuesday through Friday, from Memorial Day until Labor Day.

Memorial Day Museum, Waterloo

THINGS TO DO

Seneca Falls

64) Convention Days

The first Convention Days Celebration was held in Seneca Falls in mid-July 1979 to commemorate the first Women's Rights Convention held July 19 and 20, 1848. Convention Days celebrations include a street parade and reenactment of the 1848 Women's Rights Convention. Other activities are concerts, historical tours, five and ten kilometer races, children's activities, dancing in the park, speeches, tournaments, and a fireworks display.

65) Empire State Farm Days

Empire State Farm Days are held on more than 325 acres of the 4,000 acre Rodman Lott and Sons farm near Seneca Falls in early August. It is the major farm show in the northeast United States, with over 550 exhibits; between 75,000 and 100,000 visitors attend the three-day show each year.

Empire State Farm Days, the longest running outdoor agriculture trade show in the Northeast, began in 1933. The central focus of the show is on working farmers and the people who provide service and support to them, but there is something of interest to everyone. One of the managers of the show has observed, "Anyone who is interested in where their food and fiber comes from can learn a lot at Empire Farm Days."

The latest farm machinery is on display and Empire Farm Days provides an excellent opportunity to show children how farms are worked. Daily demonstrations of the latest agricultural techniques are given on seventy-five acres of fields. In addition to agricultural topics, such as the discussion of the latest strains of hybrid corn, a visitor has the opportunity to learn about subjects such as health and safety and the latest in profit management packages.

◆ ◆ ◆

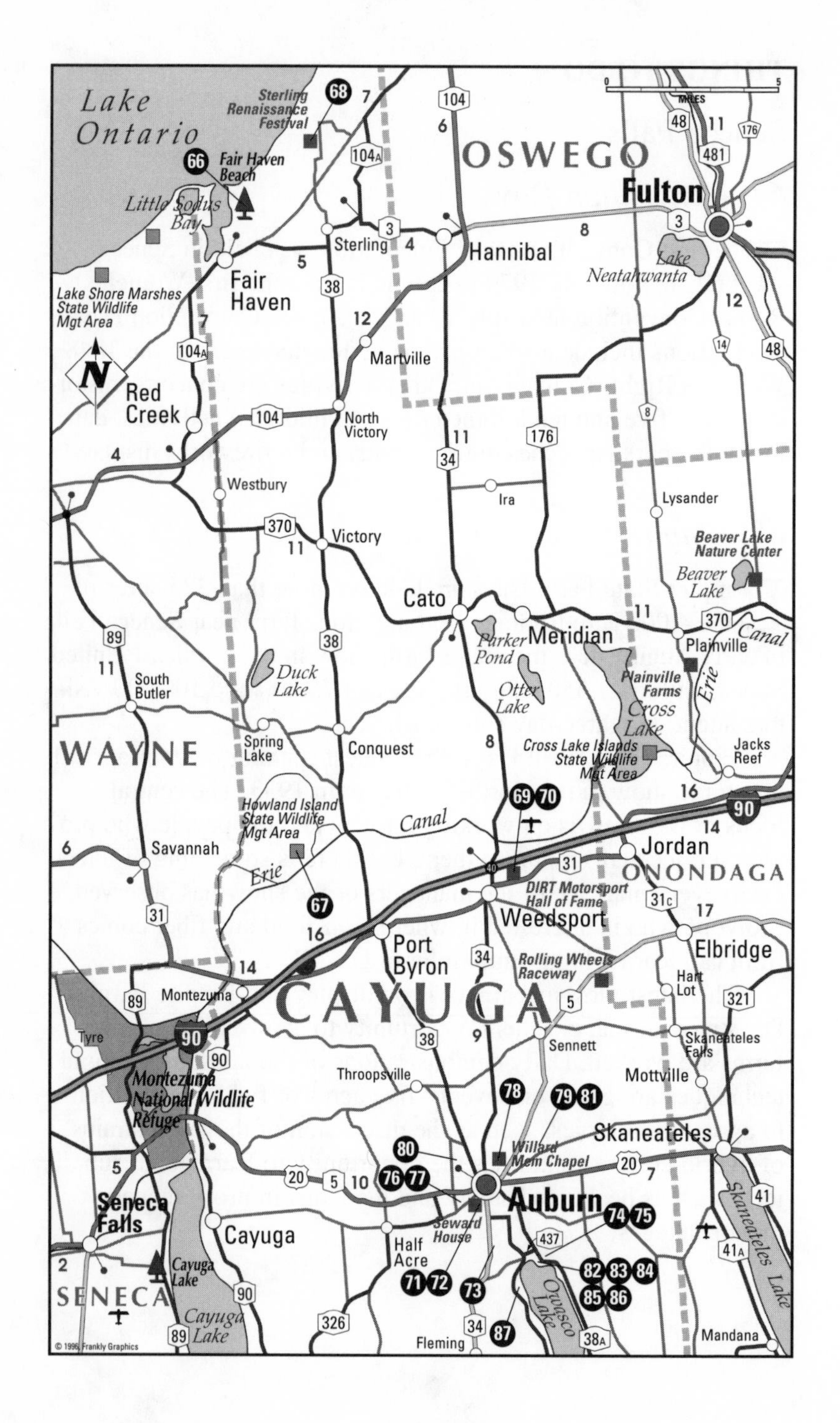
Lake Ontario
Sterling Renaissance Festival
Fair Haven Beach
Little Sodus Bay
Lake Shore Marshes State Wildlife Mgt Area
Fair Haven
Sterling
Hannibal
OSWEGO
Fulton
Lake Neatahwanta
Martville
Red Creek
North Victory
Westbury
Victory
Ira
Lysander
Beaver Lake Nature Center
Beaver Lake
Cato
Meridian
Parker Pond
Otter Lake
Plainville
Plainville Farms
Cross Lake
Erie Canal
Duck Lake
South Butler
WAYNE
Spring Lake
Conquest
Cross Lake Islands State Wildlife Mgt Area
Jacks Reef
Howland Island State Wildlife Mgt Area
Canal
Erie
Savannah
Jordan
ONONDAGA
DIRT Motorsport Hall of Fame
Weedsport
Elbridge
Port Byron
Rolling Wheels Raceway
Montezuma
CAYUGA
Hart Lot
Tyre
Sennett
Skaneateles Falls
Throopsville
Mottville
Montezuma National Wildlife Refuge
Willard Mem Chapel
Skaneateles
Auburn
Seneca Falls
Seward House
Cayuga
Half Acre
Cayuga Lake
Owasco Lake
Skaneateles Lake
SENECA
Fleming
Mandana
MILES
© 1996 Frankly Graphics

• chapter seven •

From Auburn to Lake Ontario

There is not in the wide world a valley so sweet
As that vale in whose bosom the bright waters meet;
O the last rays of feeling and life must depart
Ere the bloom of that valley shall fade from my heart.

Let the day be forever remember'd with pride
That beheld the proud Hudson to Erie allied;
O the last sand of time from His glass shall descend
Ere a union, so fruitful of glory, shall end.

From *The Meeting of the Waters*

Auburn—Brief Description and History

The City of Auburn, two and a half miles north of Owasco Lake, is a picturesque city with Historic District neighborhoods. It also has grand old homes, such as Seward House, the home of William H. Seward, Secretary of State in the administrations of Abraham Lincoln and Andrew Johnson. Auburn is located at the junction of New York State Routes 5 and 20, and is directly south of New York State Thruway Interchange 40. The city is the home of varied enterprises, including manufacturers of plastics, bottling, steel, and transportation components.

Auburn has beautiful parks, such as Emerson Park and the Casey Park family sports complex, one of Central New York's most complete outdoor recreational facilities. Fort Hill Cemetery, the site of the early Native American fort, "Osco," has a monument to Chief Logan, famed Iroquois orator. Other Auburn attractions include the the Cayuga County Agricultural Museum, Cayuga Museum with its "Home of Talking Pictures" exhibit, Schweinfurth Memorial Art Center, and the Willard Memorial Chapel, the only chapel designed by Louis Tiffany.

Captain John L. Hardenbergh, a member of the General Sullivan expedition in 1779, returned to Auburn, then Wasco, to build a log cabin and a grist mill behind the site of the present City Hall. He is known as the father of Auburn. Several mills sprang up on the Owasco Outlet, along with a stagecoach stop and tavern, and the settlement became known as Hardenbergh's Corners. In 1803, the name was changed to Auburn after "the loveliest village of the plain" in a poem by Oliver Goldsmith. By 1810, there were fourteen mills along the Owasco Outlet, including mills that made linseed oil and sunflower oil.

Auburn donated land to the State for a State prison, and construction began in September 1816. Prison reform dictated individual cells for prisoners, and Auburn prison became the first prison in the United States with a cell block. The first electric chair in the world was built at Auburn in 1890 to electrocute William Kemmler, a Buffalo murderer. Fifty-seven prisoners were electrocuted at Auburn before 1916, when executions were moved to Sing Sing. Among those executed at Auburn were Leon Czolgosz, who assassinated President McKinley at the Buffalo

Exposition in 1901, and Chester Gillette, who gained fame when his case was dramatized in Theodore Dreiser's *An American Tragedy*.

The Auburn Theological Seminary was built in 1820-21 and admitted its first students in 1821. The seminary trained Presbyterian ministers until 1939, when it was closed and merged with the Union Theological Seminary in New York City. Willard Memorial Chapel was a part of the seminary.

The first Governor of New York State from Auburn was Enos Throop, who served from 1829 to 1832. His home, Willowbrook, was built in 1818, on the east side of the lake, just south of Auburn. Willard Seward Burroughs, inventor of the first marketed adding machine, began his career as a bank clerk in Auburn. William G. Fargo, founder of the Wells Fargo Company with Henry Wells, once worked as an agent at the Auburn railroad station.

NORTH OF THE CANAL

PLACES TO SEE

66) Fair Haven Beach State Park

Fair Haven Beach State Park is located on 865 hilly, rocky acres one mile north of Fair Haven on Route 104A. Elevation in the park ranges from 245 feet to 360 feet. The park has a beautiful lakeshore, lakeshore bluffs, flat and wide expanses, inland Sterling Pond, and woodlands. Fair Haven Beach State Park contains thirty-three cabins, 191 campsites (44 electric, 147 non-electric, RVs allowed), three pavilions (two reservable), and picnic areas with tables and fireplaces. It also has playing fields, a playground, and hiking trails, including self-guided nature trails.

The park has a boat launching ramp, boat rentals, a camp store, concession stand, and pay telephones, as well as fishing, swimming at the lakeshore within the designated lifeguard area, and bathhouse facilities. There are hot showers, flush toilets, a marine sewage pumpout station, and a trailer dumping station. Camping is permitted from mid-April to the end of October; a camper recreation program is provided. The recreation building is available for use all summer and can be reserved in the off-season. Fair Haven Beach State Park is open all winter for cross-country skiing, hiking, and snowmobiling. Eight cabins with woodburning stoves are available during the winter.

Cayuga and Seneca Indians who canoed and fished on Little Sodus Bay in the mid-1600s called it "Date-ke-a-shote." In the last half of the seventeenth century, French traders used it as a landing site in trading with the Indians for furs. The French called Little Sodus Bay, "Chroutons," or passage that leads to the Cayugas. Commercial activity in the area increased significantly in 1873, when the harbor was developed and the Southern Central Railroad was completed. Coal was brought in by rail for shipment via Lake Ontario, and outgoing shipments included apples, ice, milk, and wood products.

Many cottages were built along the lake around 1900, and the area became a popular resort area. The Parks Commission was formed in 1923, and the building of park buildings and roads began in 1927; the Civilian Conservation Corps built additional buildings, campsites, roads, and trails in the 1930s.

The Park contains two examples of wave-eroded drumlins, which are hills formed by glacial drift. Beaches separate Sterling Marsh, Sterling Pond, and other backwater areas from Lake Ontario. The sheltered wetlands are home for amphibians, beavers, ducks, fish, geese, muskrats, and aquatic plants.

67) Howland Island State Wildlife Management Area

The Howland Island Wildlife Management Area, located in north central Cayuga County, three miles northwest of Port Byron, can be reached by traveling north from Port Byron to Howland Island Road. The 3,600-acre Wildlife Management Area is divided into three units: Howland Unit, 3,100 acres; Bluff Point Unit, 388 acres; and the Way-Cay Unit, 114 acres. The Erie Canal and the Seneca River are the water boundaries for Bluff Point Island and Howland Island. The topography varies from low-lying flood plains to gently rolling hills or steep drumlins.

The Wildlife Management Area contains a secondary growth of ash, basswood, black locust, hickory, oak, and willow, as well as shrubs such as alder, arrowwood, dogwood, spicebush, and sumac. Farm fields, meadows, water impoundments, wetlands, and woods provide a habitat for 220 species of birds and forty-six types of mammals, including deer, foxes, opossums, rabbits, raccoons, skunks, and squirrels.

Farmers settled Howland Island in the early 1800s and cleared the elm, maple, and oak trees to raise crops. Farming was discontinued in the 1920s; the land was idle until 1932, when it was purchased for a game refuge. The area was managed for migrating waterfowl after the Civilian Conservation Corps created 300 acres of water impoundments by constructing eighteen earthen dikes. The area has been managed primarily for the natural production of waterfowl since 1962.

Public fishing is allowed, hunting and trapping are permitted under special regulations, and waterfowl hunting is controlled via a lottery and reservation system on Howland Island. Wildlife, particularly deer, songbirds, shore birds, and waterfowl, offer the bird-watcher and photographer many opportunities. Maintenance roads are available for use as hiking trails for the bird-watcher, hiker, horseman, and naturalist. An observation tower offers a commanding view of the region. A launch site allows fishing boats access to the Erie Canal. Rules for public use:

- Howland Island Wildlife Management Area is open except from April 1 through May 31, the peak waterfowl nesting season.
- Camping is prohibited.
- Recreational boating and overnight mooring or storage of boats is not permitted.
- Off-road vehicular travel, including mopeds, motorcycles, motor scooters, snowmobiles, and trail bikes is prohibited.
- Swimming is not permitted.
- Fishing is permitted in season, except for April 1 through May 31.

THINGS TO DO

68) Sterling Renaissance Festival

The Sterling Renaissance Festival is located at 15431 Farden Road in Sterling, east of Fair Haven. It recreates festival time at the English village of Warwick during the reign of Queen Elizabeth I, about the year 1585. The comedies of Shakespeare and other playwrights of the period are performed on the Bankside Stage and Wyldwood Stage.

The festival, which was established in 1977, features period arts and crafts, entertainment, food, and music in a thirty-five-acre natural, wooded setting. The period artisans and craftspeople demonstrate the making of books, glass objects, hair garlands, wax seals and ornaments, jewelry, leather crafts, prints, and stained glass. Over fifty artisans display their crafts. The grounds are populated with beggars, jugglers, knaves, lords, ladies, minstrels, monks, puppeteers, shopkeepers, and wenches. Over 600 actors, crafters, entertainers, food service people, and gamers participate in the activities.

Visitors may come in their own Elizabethan costumes, rent costumes from the village seamstress, or stay dressed as they are. Entertainment includes fire eating, juggling, magic, music, and dancing and jousting in the lanes and on the stages. Examples of English food are fish and chips, marinated steak-on-a-stick, peasant bread, spinach pies, turkey legs, and hot apple dumplings with ice cream.

Admission is charged, but once inside the grounds there is free entertainment, outdoor theatre, and street performances, including live jousting. Other activities are Shakespearean plays, street theatre, and children's productions, such as puppet shows, storytelling, and the Theatre of Fools. Over eighty stage and street performances are ongoing at no extra charge. The season is from early July until mid-August. The day's events open with Queen Elizabeth's parade at 10:00 a.m.

SOUTH OF THE CANAL

PLACES TO SEE

Between Auburn and the Canal

69) DIRT Motorsport Hall of Fame and Classic Car Collection

The Drivers' Independent Race Tracks (DIRT) Motorsport Hall of Fame and Classic Car Museum is located at the Cayuga County Fairgrounds on Route 31, one mile from New York State Thruway Exit 40. It displays over thirty modified racing cars and more than fifty classic cars. The Hall of Fame and Museum, which opened in 1992 to preserve the history of modified dirt racing and to display classic cars, is the filming site of a weekly show that is nationally televised, "This week on DIRT."

The Jack Burgess National Parts Peddler Theatre Room shows films of old-time races. A worldwide finders' network provides classic car enthusiasts with a way of finding rare and collectible classic cars. An on-site gift shop offers apparel, collectors' items, and souvenirs. The museum is open all year; a nominal admission fee is charged.

70) Cayuga County Fair Speedway

The Cayuga County Fair Speedway is located at the Cayuga County Fairgrounds on Route 31 near Weedsport, one mile from the New York State Thruway exit 40. It is a DIRT (Drivers' Independent Race Track) track with a three-eighths-mile clay oval. Races are held every Sunday night from May through September.

Auburn

71) Fort Hill Cemetery

Fort Hill Cemetery in Auburn is the site of an earthen fort built by the Mound-builders, or Alleghans, who preceded the Cayuga Indians in the area. Their Fort Osco on the site of Fort Hill Cemetery had embankments for defense and an earthen altar for the worship of the sun. The burial mounds were outside the walls of the fortress, about 275 yards north of Fort Hill.

The Alleghan village of Osco appears to have been their easternmost settlement. Their name was given to the Allegheny Mountains and to the Allegheny River. They were driven from the region in the thirteenth century by the Iroquois.

The Cayuga village of Wasco was the birthplace in 1727 of Cayuga Chief Logan, or Tah-gah-jute, who was a celebrated orator of the Iroquois Confederacy. In 1852, a fifty-six-foot stone obelisk was erected on the site of an Alleghan altar mound in Fort Hill Cemetery in memory of Chief Logan.

Tah-gah-jute was the second son of Shikellimus, a distinguished sachem of the Cayugas, who was appointed Indian agent as a friend of the white man. Tah-gah-jute received the name of Logan when he was baptized in honor of James Logan, secretary of the province. He embraced not only Christian doctrines but also the pacificism of the Quakers. He and his wife, Alvaretta, the daughter of Ontonegea, were married by a missionary, Reverend Zeisberger.

He ceased being a pacifist when his wife and children were killed by Colonel Cresap, the English leader of a band of ruffians. Logan went on a rampage until thirty scalps hung from his belt. He made one of his more famous speeches just after this incident, in a conference with the British Governor of Virginia, at the signing of the Treaty of Lord Dunmore:

> I appeal to any white man to say if he ever entered Logan's cabin hungry and he gave him not meat; if he ever came in cold and naked, and he clothed him not. During the close of the last long and bloody war, Logan remained idle in his

> cabin, an advocate of peace. Such was my love for the whites, that my countrymen pointed, as they passed, and said, "Logan is the friend of the white men." I had even thought to have lived with you, but for the injuries of one man, Colonel Cresap, the last spring, in cold blood and unprovoked, murdered all the relations of Logan, not sparing even my wife and children.
>
> There runs not a drop of my blood in any living creature. This called on me for revenge. I have sought it. I have killed many. I have fully glutted my vengence. For my country, I rejoice at the beams of peace. But do not harbor a thought that mine is the joy of fear. Logan never felt fear. He will not turn on his heel to save his life. Who is there to mourn for Logan? Not one.

The inscription on the stone obelisk in Fort Hill Cemetery in memory of Chief Logan is from this speech, "WHO IS THERE TO MOURN FOR LOGAN."

72) The Seward House

The Seward House, located at 33 South Street, Auburn, was built in 1816-17 by Judge Elijah Miller, William H. Seward's father-in-law. The Federal-style mansion, a registered National Historic Landmark, was expanded in 1847 and in 1860. Each room in the thirty-room house, over half of which are open to the public, is furnished only with original family pieces and the gifts and memorabilia collected by William H. Seward in his travels.

The only residents of the house have been four generations of the Seward family. General William H. Seward II, a Brigadier General in the Civil War, inherited the house from his father. He headed the Auburn banking firm, William H. Seward & Company. William H. Seward III made a gift of the house, upon his death in 1951, to the Fred L. Emerson Foundation, in memory of his grandfather and father. The Foundation Historical

Association, an affiliate of the Emerson Foundation, was established to maintain and operate the house as a public museum.

William H. Seward, who was born in the hamlet of Florida, Orange County, New York, became Judge Miller's junior law partner in 1823. He graduated from Union College in 1820, continued with the study of law, and passed his bar exam before joining the law office of Judge Miller. Seward already knew the judge's daughter, Frances, since she was a schoolmate of his sister. They were married in 1824. The judge, who had been a widower since Frances was an infant, consented to the wedding on the condition that she would not leave his home while he lived. Seward, who moved into the house when they were married in 1824, once said, "I thus became an inmate of her family."

The public career of William H. Seward began with his election to the State Senate in 1830. He served two terms (1839-43) as the Governor of New York and was elected to the U.S. Senate. He was a founder of the Republican Party and was thought to be the leading Republican candidate for the Presidential nomination in 1860. However, Abraham Lincoln won the nomination and the election and asked Seward to serve as his Secretary of State. Seward continued in that cabinet position in the administration of President Andrew Johnson, after the assassination of Lincoln in 1864.

As Secretary of State, he is most frequently remembered for the purchase of Alaska from Russia for $7,000,000, or about two cents an acre. It was known as "Seward's Ice-box" or "Seward's Folly" at the time, but it is no longer viewed as a questionable purchase.

The parlor of Seward House contains the gilded furniture, upholstered with its original tapestry material, from the parlor of the Seward's Washington home. The fireplace mantel in the parlor was built by a sixteen-year-old journeyman painter and carpenter, Brigham Young, who later inherited the leadership of the Mormon Church from its founder, Joseph Smith.

The dining room table expands to seat twenty-four. Guests who were served on some of the sixty place settings of crested Imperial Sevres china, which was a gift from Prince Napoleon Bonaparte, nephew of the Emperor. The dining room also contains china that was a gift from Emperor Maximilian of Mexico and a copper samovar that was a gift from Baron Edward Stoeckl, Russian Minister to the United States, with whom Seward negotiated the purchase of Alaska.

The guests who were served in the dining room include Presidents John Quincy Adams, Martin Van Buren, Andrew Johnson, and William McKinley. Other luminaries who dined with Seward were Henry Clay, General Custer, Admiral Farragut, General Grant, and Daniel Webster.

The impressive drawing room contains many family portraits, including one of the Seward's daughter, Frances Adeline Seward, painted by Emanuel Leutze. A large painting of a Portage Falls scene by Hudson River School founder, Thomas Cole, hangs over the rosewood Steinway grand piano. Paintings by Henry Inman also hang in the mansion. The drawing room is graced by a Greek amphora, which is over 2,000 years old and was found on the island of Cyprus.

The spiral staircase leading upstairs from the front hallway was made of laurelwood and manzanita that was a gift from the California Pioneer Society. This was given in appreciation of Seward's pivotal efforts on the Senate floor in 1850 to have California admitted to the union as a free state. The staircase leads to the Diplomatic Gallery that has on display Seward's collection of over 130 prints and photographs of diplomats, generals, and world rulers.

The well-known Emanuel Leutze painting of the Alaska Purchase Treaty is prominently displayed in the gallery, as is a slender mahogany desk used by a member of the first United States Congress. That congress assembled in Federal Hall in New York City in 1789, prior to the inauguration of George Washington.

A large bust of Seward by Daniel Chester French, sculptor of the Lincoln Memorial, stands in the small north library. This library also contains the couch on which Seward was relaxing after a ride in his carriage, when he passed away about 4:00 p.m. on October 10, 1872. He had complained of having difficulty breathing.

There is also an exhibit on Harriet Tubman in Seward House.

She was a nurse, scout, and spy for the Union forces during the Civil War, and a leader of the Underground Railroad, who helped over 300 slaves escape to freedom in Canada. When she, who lived at 180 South Street, was out of town, Mrs. (Frances) Seward, also an abolitionist, hid fugitive slaves in two rooms at the back of the Seward House near the kitchen.

In addition, the Seward House has many letters, such as the one from Abraham Lincoln appointing Seward Secretary of State, original costumes dating from 1820, Civil War memorabilia, and some early Alaskan artifacts. Free guide service is available. Seward House is closed during January, February, and March.

73) Harriet Tubman House

The Harriet Tubman House is a white frame house with long verandas at 180 South Street, Auburn. Harriet Tubman personally led over 300 slaves to freedom on the Underground Railroad, which guided slaves from the South to Canada and liberation. She was also a nurse, scout, and spy for the Union forces during the Civil War.

After the Civil War, she moved to Auburn and lived in a home obtained for her by her friend, William H. Seward. Later, she came into possession of another property with twenty-six acres of land and two substantial houses. After Harriet's death, on March 10, 1913, the two houses fell into disrepair. One of the houses was taken down, and the other one was renovated by the African Methodist Episcopal Zion Church (A.M.E. Zion Church). The A.M.E. Zion Church has built a library building on the property to house much of the available reference material on Harriet Tubman.

The Harriet Tubman House is open on Tuesdays through Fridays and at other times by appointment.

74) Cayuga County Agricultural Museum

The Cayuga County Agricultural Museum is located across Route 38A from the main entrance to Emerson Park, at the northern end of Owasco Lake. The museum features farm implements dating from 1860 to 1930, the years of farming's greatest changes, and antique buggies, sleighs, and tractors. The farm equipment ranges from hand-held tools to horse-drawn tools to tractors and spans all of the major farm crops over the four seasons.

The spring wing has fitting tools and plows; the summer wing has cultivators and planters. The fall wing has corn and hay harvest equipment; the winter wing has ice-harvesting equipment and lumbering equipment. Wheat-harvesting equipment manufactured by the D. M. Osborne Company is also on display.

The Museum has a a blacksmith shop, a creamery, a general store, a veterinarian's office, a village square, and a wood and wheelwright shop, as well as a 1900 farm kitchen and an herb garden. The goal of the Museum is to take the visitor back to the rural way of life at the turn of the century. The Museum is open Saturday and Sunday afternoons in June and Wednesday through Sunday afternoons in July and August.

75) Owasco Teyetasta (Iroquois Museum)

The Owasco Teyetasta is located on Route 38A across from Emerson Park, adjacent to the Cayuga County Agricultural Museum. The Museum offers exhibits of Iroquois prehistory and history, including the Point Peninsula culture, the Owasco and Cayuga cultures, and a 12,000-year-old mastodon.

76) Cayuga Museum of History and Art

The Cayuga Museum of History and Art, located at 203 Genesee Street, Auburn, contains exhibits of historic and contemporary art and artifacts. It is housed in the mansion that was the home of Theodore Willard Case, pioneer in motion picture sound synchronization. Theodore Case and William Fox formed the Fox-Case Movietone Corporation, which became 20th Century Fox.

The museum has Indian displays and period rooms, as well as collections of domestic textiles and costumes, folk art, military and medical artifacts, and objects representative of North American industry. Local nineteenth-century artists are featured in the museum.

The Case Research Laboratory was located in Theodore Case's mansion. The sound studio was located in the carriage house. The laboratory created the first commercially successful sound-on-film system, invented by Theodore Case and E. I. Sponable. This system was used by De Forest Phonofilms Company from 1922-25 and by Fox Films from 1926-37. It predated the Warner Brothers disc system.

The Case Research Laboratory collections include the sound projector that set the standards for today's film industry, the blimp box that housed the camera man, De Forest amplifiers, experimental light cells, laboratory equipment, and Western Electric amplifiers. The collection also includes many test films made at the laboratory during the development of talking films. The museum is open Tuesday through Sunday afternoons. It is open on Monday holidays but is closed Thanksgiving Day and Christmas Day.

77) Schweinfurth Memorial Art Center

The Schweinfurth Memorial Art Center, located at 205 Genesee Street, Auburn, has exhibitions highlighting regional fine art, contemporary crafts, photography, architecture and design, and children's art. The center has a museum shop and a regional arts information center. It offers concerts, lectures, workshops, and special events.

The Art Center hosts several regionally renowned events each year, including a national Juried Quilt Show in November and December. The Art Center is open Tuesday through Friday afternoons, Sunday afternoon, and all day Saturday. In November and December, it is open Monday through Friday afternoons. Tours are available with advance notice.

78) *Willard Memorial Chapel*

The Willard Memorial Chapel, at 17 Nelson Street, Auburn, was built for the Auburn Theological Seminary in 1892-94, as a memorial to Dr. Sylvester D. Willard and his wife, Jane Frances Case, from their daughters. At the same time the chapel was being constructed, the seminary received a bequest from former Professor R. B. Welch for the construction of a new classroom building. All that remains today of the Auburn Theological Seminary is the Willard Memorial Chapel and the adjoining Welch Memorial Building, with over 8,000 feet of usable space.

The two Romanesque Revival buildings are built of gray Cayuga County limestone trimmed with red portage stone and are joined by an enclosed walkway. The architect was A. J. Warner of Rochester, and the builder was Barnes and Stout of Auburn. Both buildings are on the New York Register of Historic Places and the National Register of Historic Places. The Auburn Theological Seminary closed it doors in 1939 and became part of the Union Theological Seminary in New York City.

The Willard Memorial Chapel, which seats 250, is unique in that the entire chapel was designed by Louis Comfort Tiffany. Tiffany is known for decorating the mansions of bankers and captains of industry and, in 1881, redecorating the reception rooms of the White House. Many buildings and museums have a Tiffany lamp, plaque, or window, but the entire interior of the Willard Memorial Chapel was designed by Tiffany, including the ceiling, chairs, chandeliers, floors, glass mosaics, pews, walls, windows, and the memorial plaque. Harold Jaffe, president of the Louis Comfort Tiffany Society, calls the chapel "the only complete religious building extant in the United States designed by Louis Comfort Tiffany."

A gilt bronze and mosaic glass memorial tablet dominates the wall to the left of the entrance. It is an 18-foot by 9-foot bas-relief of an angel with extended wings in the center, looking upward toward the memorial inscription to Dr. and Mrs. Willard. St. John the Baptist and the Holy Spirit are on one side of the angel, and Hope and Charity are on the other side. The angel is holding a scroll with the inscription, "And now bideth Faith,

Willard Memorial Chapel, Auburn

Hope, and Love, these three, but the greatest of these is Love." The memorial plaque is surrounded by a border of Tiffany mosaic.

The largest Tiffany "Favrile" glass window in the chapel, directly above the memorial plaque, displays Christ sustaining St. Peter on the waves of Lake Genesareth. Tiffany derived the name "Favrile" from the Anglo-Saxon word for "handmade." Nine "Mooresque" style chandeliers designed by Tiffany hang from the vaulted wood ceiling. They are made of jeweled and leaded glass, mounted in bronze, and have crystal pendants hanging from them.

There is a row of seven oak chairs, inlaid with glass and metal mosaic, behind the carved oak / gold stenciled pulpit. Singing in the chapel was accompanied by a large Steere and Turner tracker organ. Other features of the chapel include fourteen opalescent windows, mosaic floors, and oak wainscoting.

One well-known family associated with the Auburn Theological Seminary was the Dulles family. Reverend Allen Macy Dulles moved to Auburn with his family in 1904 to teach at the seminary, and to serve as pastor of the Second Presbyterian Church. One of Reverend Dulles' sons, John Foster Dulles, served as Secretary of State and another son, Allen Welch Dulles, was the Director of the Central Intelligence Agency.

The interior of the chapel was almost auctioned off in the late 1980s, but was saved by the Community Preservation Committee of Auburn. The Seventh Day Adventist Church, owners of the chapel from 1957 until 1988, decided to build a new church that would be more economical to heat. The chapel was sold to an antique dealer, who planned to dismantle and sell the interior. However, the preservation committee prevailed upon him to sell the chapel to them for $500,000 (even though Tiffany lamps sold for $480,000 in 1987).

The Community Preservation Committee plans to continue the chapel's use as a place of interfaith worship and as a setting for functions such as concerts and weddings. Tours are conducted on Tuesday through Friday afternoons (and by appointment) that focus on its art, architecture, and history. The chapel doesn't provide tours during January, February, and March. A 22-minute video, "The Willard Memorial Chapel Story," traces the history of the chapel from its beginning as a part of the Auburn Theological Seminary.

79) Cayuga Community College

Cayuga Community College, founded in 1953, is a two-year college sponsored by Cayuga County and supervised by the State University of New York. The college is located on a 40.6-acre campus at 197 Franklin Street, Auburn, and has over 2,700 full-time and part-time students. The college is known for its strong liberal arts programs and a number of technology programs, several of which have been developed at the college, including computer technology / telecommunications and radio / television technology.

The college has a computer assisted drawing (CAD) lab, a fully equipped color television studio, a campus pre-school center, and a passive solar heated classroom building. The Norman F. Bourke Memorial Library has over 75,000 volumes, over 600 periodicals, many Federal and New York State documents, and an extensive pamphlet file. The library also has a comprehensive collection of prints, films, audiotapes, videotapes, filmstrips, slides, phonograph records, and compact discs. The campus has a $3.2 million dollar health / physical education / recreation facility and an exercise circuit / nature trail. Students interested in art and drama find abundant on-campus and community offerings.

80) Casey Park

Casey Park is a 44-acre family sports complex located on N. Division Street in Auburn. It has an olympic swimming pool and a mini-pool, a soccer field, basketball courts, tennis courts, platform tennis courts, and two softball fields with lights. It also has an outdoor amphitheatre, bike trails, fitness trails, bocce courts, horseshoe pits, picnic areas, and a playground.

Casey Park has an indoor artificial ice skating rink that is open from November to April. The park is open year-round; it is one of Central New York's most complete recreation areas.

81) Cayuga Community College Nature Trail

The Cayuga Community College Nature Trail is a mile-long exercise and nature trail located in the northeast corner of the campus. A self-administered exercise program is available at nine exercise stations. A pond is located along the trail; the many trees and wildflowers are maintained for study by botany and conservation students. The entrance to the trail is off Franklin Street, Auburn.

82) Emerson Park

Emerson Park, an Auburn City Park at the northern end of Owasco Lake, is the principal access point for the lake. It is located on Route 38A, just south of Auburn. The park has a swimming beach, picnic facilities, playgrounds, a ballroom, a pavilion, and children's rides, including a carousel. The Merry-Go-Round Playhouse is located in the park. The Cayuga County Agriculture Museum is located directly across Route 38A from the main entrance to the park.

The park also has canoe and paddleboat rentals and a public boat launch. Emerson Park has extensive lawns along the lake, and there is fishing for bass, perch, northern pike, and lake trout.

THINGS TO DO

83) Auburn Concert Series

The Syracuse Symphony performs a concert series in Auburn each year. Concert selections include classics, opera, and pops. The Symphony also provides summer concerts in Emerson Park along the lakefront.

84) Merry-Go-Round Playhouse

The Merry-Go-Round Playhouse, which opened in 1959, is a non-profit regional theatre that presents musical, contemporary, and youth productions. The Playhouse, a showcase for professional repertory theatre, offers musicals from June to late August. The 328-seat theatre, the largest of its kind in Central New York, is located in Emerson Park, on the lakefront.

85) Antique / Classic Boat Show

The Antique / Classic Boat Show, which began in Auburn in 1987, is held in late July or early August in Emerson Park, Route 38A, just south of Auburn, along the northern end of Owasco Lake. Owners bring over fifty antique / classic boats, with their polished brass and varnished mahogany or teak, from the Northeast, the Midwest, and Canada. One-of-a-kind canoes, rowboats, old launches, steamboats, runabouts, and rum runners from the Thousand Islands have been entered in past shows. Awards are given in a traditional ceremony.

An example of an entry in earlier shows is the 1915 Ingeson steam launch Eagle. The slender, 21-foot craft, with its red and white striped canopy, was one of the most popular boats in the show as it cruised the lake accompanied by a steady hiss of steam and an occasional blast from its highly polished brass whistle.

In previous shows, there has been a chicken barbecue on Saturday afrernoon and a pancake breakfast on Sunday morning. On both days of the show, the children's rides (including a carousel) at Emerson Park are open, and there is swimming off the sandy beaches. Canoes and paddleboats are available for rental.

86) Finger Lakes Antique Car Show

The Finger Lakes Antique Car Show is held in late July at Emerson Park, Route 38A, just south of Auburn. The show has over 400 entries from the United States and Canada.

87) Springside Inn—Historic Restaurant and Inn

The Springside Inn is located on Route 38, on the west side of Owasco Lake, just south of Auburn. It is a fine restaurant, a bed and breakfast inn, and an outstanding location for special events. The Springside Inn also offers packages for executive groups, including a lunch / meeting package and a dinner / meeting package.

The main public dining room, the Surrey Room, has an old-world charm, enhanced by its massive beams, cathedral ceiling, turn-of-the-century hanging lamps, and stone fireplace. On Sundays, the Springside Inn offers brunch from late morning until early afternoon and a family dinner. The family dinner (on which the Springside claims their reputation was built) is a feast of baked chicken, roast beef, and baked Virginia ham, with all of the trimmings, including cheese souffle and make-your-own sundaes with homemade sauces. The regular menu is also available on Sunday.

In 1851, the Reverend Samuel Robbins Brown, pastor of the Dutch Reformed Church of the Owasco Outlet (Sand Beach Church), opened a school at the Springside Inn, and called it the "Springside" school. In 1858, Dr. Brown became the first American missionary to Japan. An assistant ran the school until 1867, when it was sold to become a private residence.

In the 1800s, the Springside was used as a station on the Underground Railroad, for slaves escaping from the South to freedom in Canada. The Springside passed though several owners and was purchased in 1919 by Captain John A. Holland, an Englishman marrried to a MacDougall from Auburn. The Hollands ran it as a summer resort until the 1940s, when it became a year-round hotel / restaurant.

In 1941, the Stephen J. Miller family purchased the Springside Inn. The second generation of the Miller family continued the operation of the Inn.

◆ ◆ ◆

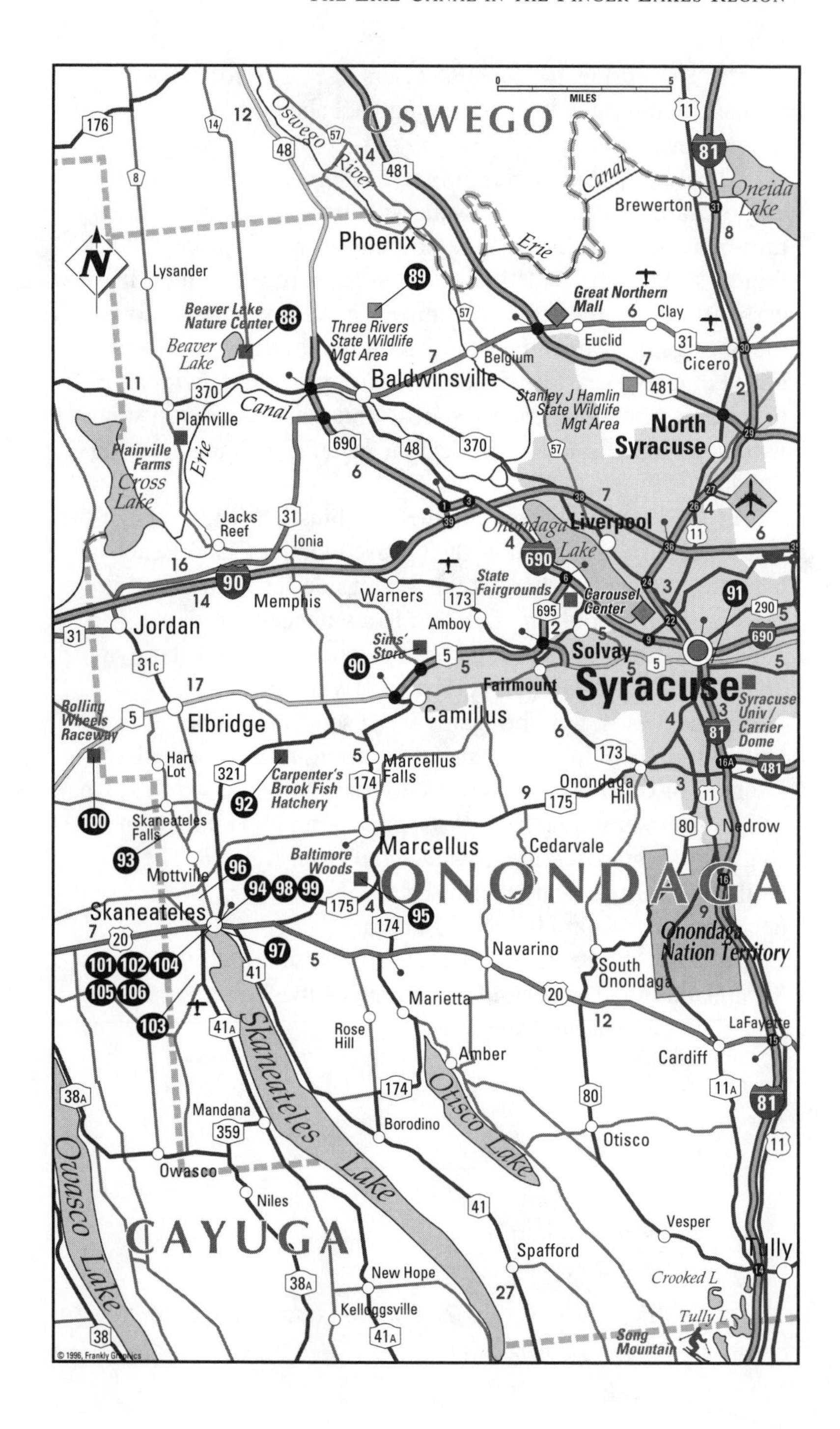
OSWEGO
ONONDAGA
CAYUGA
Syracuse
North Syracuse
Liverpool
Solvay
Phoenix
Baldwinsville
Jordan
Elbridge
Camillus
Marcellus
Skaneateles
Erie Canal
Oneida Lake
Onondaga Lake
Cross Lake
Beaver Lake
Skaneateles Lake
Otisco Lake
Owasco Lake
Beaver Lake Nature Center
Three Rivers State Wildlife Mgt Area
Great Northern Mall
Stanley J Hamlin State Wildlife Mgt Area
State Fairgrounds
Carousel Center
Sims' Store
Plainville Farms
Rolling Wheels Raceway
Carpenter's Brook Fish Hatchery
Baltimore Woods
Syracuse Univ / Carrier Dome
Onondaga Nation Territory
Song Mountain
MILES
© 1996, Frankly Graphics

• chapter eight •

From Skaneateles to Oswego County

John Mueller was a mule-driver
On Erie's verdant shore,
His walk was humble, but his gait
Was something to adore.

The lockman's daughter
Had for him a passion strong;
Athough she was both short and small,
She vowed she'd love him long.

Her father's haughty castle
Stood beside the proud Mohawk;
He did not lock her in the keep,
But kept her in the lock.

From *The Ballad of John Mueller and the Lock Tender's Daughter*

Skaneateles—Brief Description and History

The village of Skaneateles, located at the northern end of Skaneateles Lake, has a population of over 8,000, and is known for its award-winning downtown. The village boasts of preserved homes and shops, a scenic setting on the lake, and good restaurants, such as the Krebs and the Sherwood Inn. Some people spell the name of the village "SkanEATeles."

The village has Austin and Thayer parks, the John D. Barrow Art Gallery, scenic cruises from the foot of the lake, Polo on Sunday afternoons during July and August, the Skaneateles Nature Trail, and band concerts in Thayer Park. Other activities include weekly sailboat races with regattas on Fourth of July and Labor Day weekends, "flares around the lake" on July 3rd, and antique shows, art exhibits, and flower shows.

The Skaneateles Festival, a high-quality regional chamber music festival with approximately eighty musicians, is held each year during August. Nearby is the Baltimore Woods nature preserve and an operating water-driven flour mill at New Hope, about two miles from the west shore of the southern end of the lake.

The first non-Native American visitors to the site of the village, Moravian missionaries, came from Bethlehem, Pennsylvania, in 1750. They built "the Pilgrim's Hut" of logs on St. James Beach, near the current location of St. James Episcopal Church. The first settlers on the site of the village were Abraham Cuddleback, his wife, and their eight children, who arrived after a forty-three-day wagon trip from Orange County.

By 1797, a series of mills using the outlet for power had been built along Skaneateles Creek, in Skaneateles, Mottville, and Skaneateles Falls. An artisan from Salem, Massachusetts, brought the New England influence to the architecture of the older homes in the village. He lived in Skaneateles from 1812 to 1820, and built many of the "Salem doorways" that still decorate many of the older houses.

Isaac Sherwood was an early settler who delivered mail on foot, then on horseback, and founded a stage coach company, the Old Mail Line, in 1809. The company had the contract for carrying mail between Utica and Canandaigua. By 1815, he had fifteen stage coaches in service passing through Skaneateles and stopping at the original 1807 Sherwood Inn.

Skaneateles was a stop on the Underground Railroad during the mid-1800s. Evergreen House at 98 West Genessee Street was a rest stop for slaves being escorted from the South to freedom in Canada. People who lived in the Skaneateles area in its early days include Henry Arnold, brother of General Benedict Arnold, the Revolutionary War traitor, and two members of the Roosevelt family, Nicholas and S. Montgomery Roosevelt. Henry Roosevelt, owner of a summer home on the lake, served in the Department of the Navy with his relative, Assistant Secretary of the Navy Franklin Delano Roosevelt.

In 1899, Skaneateles native son Fred C. Krebs and his wife, Cora, began serving meals to neighbors and then opened a small restaurant. By 1915, the Krebs Restaurant expanded to be able to serve 3,000 meals on Saturdays and Sundays during the summer. The Krebs has been in the family through three generations.

NORTH OF THE CANAL

PLACES TO SEE

88) Beaver Lake Nature Center

Beaver Lake Nature Center, located two miles west of Route 370 on East Mud Lake Road, is a major resting place for thousands of Canada geese in the spring and the fall. The nature center has a 200-acre lake, which can be viewed from a floating boardwalk, and miles of woodland trails for cross-county skiing and hiking. The Center provides interpretive programs presented by professional naturalists to aid in exploring the natural world. Visitors can also learn from state-of-the-art exhibits in the modern visitor center.

89) Three Rivers State Wildlife Management Area

Three Rivers Wildlife Management Area, located north of Skaneateles between Baldwinsville and Phoenix, is a 3,497-acre tract that provides a habitat for over 118 species of birds, including bald eagles, blue herons, Canada geese, and osprey. Access is from Route 48; Kellogg Road and Potter Road traverse the Wildlife Management Area. Three Rivers Wildlife Management Area was named "Three Rivers" because it is near the site where the the Oneida and Seneca Rivers form the Oswego River. The Wildlife Management Area is flat and poorly drained.

The Area has brushlands, open areas, wetlands, and woodlands that provide habitats for eight species of amphibians, eleven species of fish, twenty-five species of mammals, and six species of reptiles. Aspen, beech, birch and sugar maple trees grow in the drier areas, and ash, hemlock, red maple, and white pine in the lowlands. Plantation conifers such as larch, Norway spruce, white spruce, and red, white, and Scots pine are also found in the area. Over 50,000 evergreens and shrubs provide cover and food for wildlife.

Since 1950, pheasant retriever trial areas have been maintained for training bird dogs. National and local events are held each year, with dogs, owners, and trainers attending from North America and from several foreign countries. Field trials are open to the public.

Fishing, hunting, and trapping are allowed in the Wildlife Management Area. Hunting, which is controlled under state regulations, is for deer, pheasants, rabbits, ruffed grouse, squirrels, and waterfowl. Fishing access to the Oswego River is provided on an undeveloped site. Maintenance roads and town roads provide access to the area for birding, bicycling, cross-country skiing, horseback riding, and nature study.

Educational outings are allowed by permit Individual camping is prohibited in the Three Rivers Wildlife Management Area. Boating, swimming, and overnight mooring and storage of boats are not permitted. The use of off-road vehicles is prohibited except on town and county roads.

SOUTH OF THE CANAL

PLACES TO SEE

East of Skaneateles

90) Camillus Erie Canal Park

Camillus Erie Canal Park, located on Devoe Road in Camillus, is a 300-acre park with seven miles of navigable canal and towpath trails. The Lock Tender's Shanty Museum and the Sims Store Museum, located at "Camillus Landing," are authentic replicas of actual buildings; they contain artifacts, memorabilia, and photographs of the Erie Canal. The Nine Mile Creek Aqueduct is within the park, along with flower gardens, nature trails, and picnic areas.

The Sims Store Museum is the point of departure for boat rides on the canal, which are offered on Sunday afternoons from May through October. The park is open daily year-round. Tours of the park are given by appointment.

91) Erie Canal Museum

The Erie Canal Museum, located at 318 Erie Boulevard in Syracuse, is the leading maritime museum specializing in Erie Canal History in the United States. The museum is housed in the 1850 Weighlock Building, which has been restored to its appearance of the 1850s. The Weighlock Building, the only surviving canalboat weighing station on the Erie Canal and a National Historic Landmark, weighed boats of up to 100 feet in length.

Visitors to the Museum can explore the history of Syracuse as it grew from a salt marsh to a city. They can also board a 65-foot canal boat, the *Frank Thomson*, to experience life and work on the Erie Canal. The Education Gallery has historic stereoviews of the Erie Canal, live demonstrations, period room settings, and participatory exhibits that allow the visitor to operate a bilge pump and to try on a diving helmet. Special exhibitions showcase the Museum's collections of canalboat models, china, costumes, and patent models. The orientation theatre provides an overview of the history of the world's most successful canal, which was the only water route through the Appalachian Mountains.

The Museum's research library is open to the public by appointment. The Erie Canal Museum offers a gift shop, group tours, a speaker's bureau, and videotape rentals. The Museum also provides current information on the cultural and educational activities available throughout the New York State Canal System. The Museum is open Tuesday through Sunday year-round; it is closed Mondays, Thanksgiving Day, Christmas Day, and New Year's Day.

Between Skaneateles and the Canal

92) Carpenter's Brook Fish Hatchery

Carpenter's Brook Fish Hatchery, which is located approximately eight miles north of Skaneateles on Route 321, is open for tours and has a special 16-foot by 24-foot children's fish pool and traveling display. The Hatchery produces more than 100,000 brook trout, brown trout, rainbow trout, and walleye pike annually. It has a picnic area with tables and benches.

93) Wooden Toy Factory

The t. c. timber factory (formerly Skaneateles Handicrafters) is at 4407 Jordan Road between Mottville and Skaneateles Falls, several miles north of Skaneateles. Marshall Larrabee, the founder of Skaneateles Handicrafters, did not intend to spend his life being a toy maker; he thought he was going to be a banker. He graduated from the University of Pennsylvania's Wharton School of Business during the Depression and accepted a position at the Trust & Deposit Bank in Syracuse.

The following year, shortly after marrying his wife, Elizabeth, he was told that he had tuberculosis. There were no drugs to treat the disease in the 1930s, so he spent the next ten years in bed. As soon as he could spend a few minutes a day out of bed, he asked for a band saw, a circular saw, a drill press, and a lathe. Elizabeth had challenged him to build a small train that a child could hold in his or her hand. Their daughter, Ethel, received the first train that Marshall made, and it was a hit.

For the next several years, Larrabee made thirty small trains as Christmas gifts for the children of their friends and neighbors. In 1940, Marshall took a box filled with his wooden trains to Chicago to talk with the senior buyer at Marshall Fields. She said that she would buy all that he could make. Over the next forty years, the work force increased from two, Marshall and Elizabeth, to over 100 employees.

Their first trains included an engine, coach, flat car, and tank car, connected with hooks and eyes from the local hardware store. Maple was used because it is a fine-grained wood that is easy to work, and it does not sliver easily. Also, it is readily available in the southern tier of New York State and the northern tier of Pennsylvania.

Marshall Larrabee sold the business in 1980. It is now called t. c. timber, and is owned by Habermaas, a German company. The wooden toys are still made as Marshall made them, except that the hooks and eyes that used to connect the cars of the trains are now small magnets. An outlet store is operated by t. c. timber at the factory.

Skaneateles

94) Austin Park

Austin Park, on Austin Street in Skaneateles, has baseball fields, basketball courts, picnic areas, and tennis courts, all with outdoor lighting for evening use. Allyn Arena in the park provides artificial ice for general skating, figure skating, and hockey for six months of the year.

95) Baltimore Woods

Baltimore Woods is a 160-acre nature preserve located in rolling hills one mile south of the village of Marcellus, about six miles northeast of Skaneateles. The nature preserve is on the west side of Bishop Hill Road, which runs between Marcellus and Route 20. Baltimore Woods has a pavilion, log cabin, herb garden, wildflower garden, and four miles of self-guided trails. The only indoor facility is a small meeting room.

Baltimore Woods is owned by Save the County, an organization founded in 1971 to preserve the green spaces of Onondaga County. Several trails are maintained throughout the year, and are open to the public at all times. Volunteer naturalists conduct guided tours upon request.

Programs offered by the nature preserve include a Fall Festival, Maple Syrup Festival, summer day nature program for children, teacher workshops, and a volunteer naturalist program. Baltimore Woods also has Friday Night Nature Walks, Herb Sale Day, visits by naturalists to schools, school visits to the center, and many other seasonal programs.

96) Skaneateles Nature Trail

The Skaneateles Nature Trail follows Skaneateles Creek, just north of the village of Skaneateles. Skaneateles Creek flows northward from Skaneateles to the Seneca River / Erie Canal; it empties into the canal near Cross Lake.

97) Thayer Park

Thayer Park is a pleasant village park along Genesee Street (Route 20) in Skaneateles, which offers scenic views of the northern end of Skaneateles Lake and of the beautiful homes on the slopes of the west side of the lake. During the summer, band concerts are presented at the gazebo, and the park features craft fairs and outdoor art shows.

98) John D. Barrow Art Gallery

The John D. Barrow Art Gallery adjoins the village of Skaneateles Library, and admittance to the gallery is through the library. The gallery displays over 300 oil paintings by John Barrow in two exhibition rooms. Some of Barrow's smaller paintings are mounted on special frames on the lower walls of the gallery, serving as striking wainscoting.

John Barrow moved to Skaneateles with his family when he was fourteen, was sent to England for his education, and returned to Skaneateles at the age of nineteen. He lived twenty years of his adulthood in New York City to be near other artists, but spent most of his life in Skaneateles, where he died at the age of eighty-two in 1906.

Barrow was a member of the Hudson River School of painters and is considered one of America's "second generation" of landscape painters. Most of his paintings were of landcapes, including many of the Finger Lakes Region, but he was also a portrait painter. His well-known portrait of Abraham Lincoln is currently owned and displayed by the Chicago Historical Society.

The village of Skaneateles Library is a gray stone building on East Genesee Street that originally served as a law office. John Barrow financed an annex to the library building in 1900 to be used as a gallery to exhibit his art. By 1970, the gallery became rundown and had to be closed. Through the efforts of the Skaneateles Historical Society and art-oriented townspeople, $40,000 was collected to renovate the gallery. It was reopened in 1977.

Since 1977, over 100 severely damaged paintings have been restored with the help of local groups and individuals. The restoration work continues. The gallery is operated by a management committee and dedicated volunteers. A unique feature of the gallery is that it displays most of the lifetime output of one artist.

99) Skaneateles Historical Association Museum—The Creamery

The Skaneateles Historical Society Museum, located at 28 Hannum Street, was previously the Skaneateles Creamery Company's creamery building, which was given to the village of Skaneateles in 1989. The Historical Society renovated the building and opened the Museum in 1992.

The Museum houses hundreds of local artifacts, a gift shop, and a meeting room used by the Historical Society and other local organizations. The expanding archives and research department includes photo and newspaper files, biographical records, and cemetery records. The Museum also has many permanent exhibits, including a fascinating display on the area's teasel (a thistle-like plant used to produce a napped surface on fabrics) industry, as well as changing displays.

The Skaneateles Historical Society museum is open year-round on Friday afternoons and on Thursday and Saturday afternoons during the summer.

THINGS TO DO

Between Skaneateles and the Canal

100) Rolling Wheels Track

The Rolling Wheels Track is located on Route 5 in Elbridge, north of Skaneateles. It is a Drivers' Independent Race Track (DIRT) track with a five-eighths-mile clay oval. The track is open from April to September.

Skaneateles

101) Skaneateles Art Exhibition

The Skaneateles Art Exhibition is held in October at several sites in the village. Paintings, sculptures, and ceramics are on exhibit throughout Skaneateles. Music and dance performances are also scheduled during the week of the exhibition.

102) The Skaneateles Festival

The Skaneateles Festival is a regional chamber music festival that began in 1980 and offers a four-week season during the month of August. The fest is a combination of work and play for the approximately eighty musicians who live together at Brook Farm or stay as guests in other private homes. Many bring spouses, children, and friends with them.

The musicians rehearse during the week and give three concerts each week: Thursday and Friday evenings at St. James Episcopal Church, 94 East Genesee Street, and Saturday evenings at Brook Farm, weather permitting. For a stage, the musicians use the veranda of the beautiful house with the tall, white pillars. Seating is on the lawn at Brook Farm and concertgoers bring their own lawn chairs and blankets. The concerts are moved to St. Mary's of the Lake Church, 81 Jordan Street, Skaneateles, in inclement weather.

Two of the founders of the festival are David and Louise Robinson, owners of Brook Farm. Most of the work in organizing the event is done throughout the year by a core group of people who serve on committees and on the board of directors. The festival, which was once known as the "best kept secret in the East" has gained a national reputation.

The organizers have no difficulty attracting talented musicians to the festival. It is a small, intimate festival that provides an opportunity for interaction between the concertgoers and the musicians. Composers are encouraged to attend the festival to give the musicians and the audiences a chance to met them and to learn more about their work.

103) Skaneateles Polo Club

The Skaneateles Polo Club plays at 3:00 p.m. every Sunday in July and August at a playing field on Andrews Road, just west of the intersection of Andrews Road and West Lake Road (Route 41A). The game is played rain or shine, but play is discontinued if the field becomes slippery. It is played with two teams of four players each on a field three times as long and three times as wide as a football field.

The game consists of hitting a hard, white three-inch ball at speeds approaching 100 miles per hour with a four-foot cane mallet, while riding a polo pony at up to forty-five miles a hour. The duration of the game is forty-five minutes, made up of six periods (chukkers) of seven and a half minutes each. An announcer describes the plays.

The polo ponies are thoroughbreds, quarterhorses, or mixed thoroughbred / quarter horses. The intensity of the game is such that one pony has the energy for about two chukkers; most players ride three ponies per match. Serious riders have four, five, or six ponies available for each match. Polo ponies are selected based on agility, courage, endurance, speed, and temperament; it takes at least two years to train one thoroughly.

Polo is considered to be a contact sport, but the fact that the rules are designed to protect the horse takes some of the danger out of the game. Riders are allowed to bump another horse to spoil a shot, but if the opponent's horse is knocked off balance, a "dangerous riding" foul is called.

The word polo is a derivation of the Tibetan word for ball, "pulu." Its place of origin is uncertain, but it was played in Persia over twelve centuries ago. The Chinese claim that their ancestors played polo in 1000 BC. Initially, it was more of a conditioning for war than a game. The Arabs learned the game from the Persians; later, it became popular in Greece, India, and England.

James Gordon Bennett, Jr., owner and editor of the New York *Herald*, introduced polo to the United States in 1876, the year of the first championship game. Harvard was the first college to have an organized polo team, and the U.S. Polo Association was formed in 1890. Polo was once considered to be the sport of royalty, or of wealthy people, but there are now over 225 polo clubs in the United States with a total membership of more than 2,200 players. Many players learn the game in college or at polo clinics.

The Skaneateles Polo Club was formed in 1962 by Donald H. Cross, Tim Gridley, and Peter J. Winkelman. In recent years, matches have attracted crowds of 200 to 300 spectators. It is a pleasant way to spend a Sunday afternoon, while watching the action from a lawn chair, socializing, and sharing a picnic lunch.

104) Mid-Lakes Navigation Ltd. Cruises

Mid-Lakes Navigation Co., Ltd., 11 Jordan Street, Skaneateles, has been offering Skaneateles Lake cruises since 1968. Their original dinner cruise is a three-hour cruise on a classic wooden boat, the *Barbara S. Wiles*, or the double-decked sixty-foot *Judge Ben Wiles,* with its mahogany trim and brass fittings.

The Sunday Brunch Cruise excursion is a three-hour cruise with a hearty brunch fare; the luncheon cruise (Monday through Friday) is a two-hour cruise. Both are on the *Judge Ben Wiles.* Mid-Lakes Navigation also offers one-hour cruises on the *Judge Ben Wiles* on Monday through Friday and on the *Barbara S. Wiles* on Saturday and Sunday.

A thirty-two-mile U.S. mailboat cruise, which lasts three and a half hours, is provided daily, except Sundays and holidays, on the *Barbara S. Wiles*. Mail is delivered to cottages around the lake on this cruise, one of the last water routes for mail delivery in the U.S. When Captain Peter Wiles took over the mail route in 1968, the route had been in operation for over 100 years, going back to the time of the steamboats on Skaneateles Lake.

The Boat Works of Mid-Lakes Navigation is located at the top of Bockes Road, off Route 41 in Borodino, eight miles south of Skaneateles, on the east side of the lake. Mid-Lakes Navigation also provides Erie Canal and Onondaga Lake cruises. It is a family business run by the Wiles family.

Mid-Lakes Navigation, Ltd., also offers cruises that originate in Syracuse and pass through the area north of the lakes. The Syracuse to Buffalo cruise on the 40-passenger *Emita II* departs from Cold Springs Harbor near Syracuse. Highlights of the cruise include

- the Montezuma National Wildlife Refuge and six locks
- docking at Newark—overnight lodging nearby
- stopping at Palmyra to inspect the 1825 aqueduct
- docking at Brockport's Harvester Park—overnight lodging nearby
- Medina Aqueduct and double locks at Lockport
- docking at North Tonawanda—return to Syracuse by chartered motorcoach

Tour Boats on Skaneateles Lake

In addition, Mid-Lakes Navigation offers cruises from Buffalo to Syracuse, Syracuse to Albany, and Albany to Syracuse via the Erie Canal on the *Emita II*. They offer cruises on Onondaga Lake and the Erie Canal near Syracuse on the *City of Syracuse*. Mid-Lakes Navigation also rents Lockmaster Hireboats on the Erie Canal.

105) The Krebs—Historic Restaurant

The Krebs, located at 53 West Genesee Street, has been in continual operation, May through October, since 1899. In 1899, Fred R. Krebs and his wife, Cora, began to serve three meals a day to their neighbors for $8.00 a week. They soon expanded to a small restaurant with a capacity of twenty-five patrons. By 1915, customers either had to make reservations or wait two hours to be served. In 1920, the Krebs was serving 3,000 meals on Saturdays and Sundays during the summer, and was operating at capacity for the rest of the week.

The restaurant, which has a capacity of 150, is located in a large white frame house that has been expanded several times. From a description of The Krebs in their wine list:

> There are no menus used at The Krebs—instead we feature our traditional meal which includes a first course (fresh fruit cup, shrimp cocktail, tomato juice, melon), a choice of soup (clear broth or creamed soup), lobster a la newburg (made from Mrs. Krebs' secret recipe). [Other courses include] English sliced roast prime rib, pan fried half broilers of chicken, white potatoes, candied sweet potatoes, fresh vegetable, beef gravy, creamed mushrooms, and toast points, sweet rolls, and a choice of homemade sweet rolls and ice cream. Also included are a choice of salads, relishes, homemade bread and rolls, and a platter of brownies and angel food cake accompanies all desserts.

> Two smaller meals are also offered for those who feel that they cannot do justice to a full seven-course meal. The format of these two [four-course] meals is basically the same as the traditional meal but slightly abbreviated to please the lighter appetite. One features the lobster a la newburg, served with a side of wild rice, and the other, the roast prime rib and chicken entrees. A children's menu is also available. Vegetables and desserts change with the seasons and availability. All food is prepared on the premises, the emphasis being placed on quality.
>
> The Krebs Original Sunday Brunch is served every Sunday during the season and consists of a choice of first course (fresh fruit cup, juices, and melon in season), choice of cereal or French onion soup, creamed chicken and baking powder biscuits, scrambled eggs and sausage, roast beef hash, sweet rolls, muffins, and hot pop-overs. There are homemade jams or jellies on the table and coffee is served constantly. To top off the brunch, there are waffles served with hot syrup and sherbet.

In 1946, the upstairs living quarters of Mr. and Mrs. Krebs were converted into sitting rooms and a cocktail lounge and furnished with Early American Tavern furniture. The restaurant is furnished with antiques, with linen tablecloths and fresh flowers on the tables and lace curtains in the windows. The Krebs has attempted, successfully, to keep the restaurant the way it was in the early 1900s. The restaurant has been the Krebs family through three generations.

106) The Sherwood Inn— Historic Restaurant and Inn

The Sherwood Inn, located at 26 West Genesee Street, Skaneateles, was built as a stage coach stop and tavern in 1807. The Inn has twenty guest rooms / suites, all with telephones and private baths, and many have a view of the northern end of Skaneateles Lake. The Sherwood Inn has an extensive menu that offers American cooking with a continental touch.

The Inn has several formal dining rooms and a summer dining area on a screened-in porch where diners can watch the sailboats on the lake. Casual fare is served in their tavern in a friendly atmosphere that is mixed with jazz on Sunday afternoons. The Inn has ample conference rooms to accommodate business guests, including a cherry-panelled room adjacent to the main dining room and the West Porch.

The attractive lobby has a fireplace and is furnished with Stickley furniture, a baby grand piano, and oriental carpets. Antiques and period furnishings from the early 19th century through Victorian times provide a decor that is consistent with the Inn's past. The Inn has a small library and "the Boat," a restored 1946 Chris Craft, which can be reserved by guests for rides on the lake.

◆ ◆ ◆

Sherwood Inn, Skaneateles

Epilogue

"The legislature hereby finds and declares that the New York State Canal System is one of the state's greatest assets ... it is essential that the beauty, historic character, and environmental integrity of the canals be preserved for future generations ... the commission shall develop a conceptual framework for fostering the development of the canal system into a canal recreationway system...."

New York State Legislature—Chapter 766 of the Laws of 1992, as amended

The Future of the Erie Canal

The Erie Canal is, in fact, one of New York State's greatest assets, and the state, county, and local governments as well as other organizations are promoting its use as a recreationway system and preserving it for future generations. In 1992, the New York State Legislature enacted "Thruway 2000" legislation that transferred the Canal System from the Department of Transportation to the Thruway Authority and established the Canal Corporation as a wholly owned subsidiary of the Thruway Authority to operate, preserve, and renew the Canal System for recreation and economic development.

In July 1995, a major step in implementing canal plans was taken when Peter Tufo, chairman of the New York State Canal Recreationway Commission, submitted the "New York State Recreationway Plan" to the New York State Thruway Authority and the New York State Canal Corporation. Tufo was also the chairman of the New York Canal Commission, which included members William C. Warren III of Pittsford and Nancy E. Carey of Albany. In announcing the plan, Tufo stated that "the plan is a vision for a reinvigorated Canal System which will foster economic and cultural development in communities across the state."

The three fundamental goals of the Canal Recreationway Plan are to preserve the best of the past, to enhance recreational opportunities, and to foster economic development. The plan includes provisions for the preservation and enhancement of historic buildings, sites, and districts as well as for encouraging the use of historic buildings, sites, and districts listed on or eligible for the State or National Registers of Historic Places.

In order to enhance recreational opportunities, the plan provides for the formulation of an integrated boating system with charter routes, cruise ships, dinner boats, expanded boater services, mixed-use terminal locations, tourist accommodations, and support facilities.

The plans for economic development include:

- Promotion of economic development and tourism in cities, hamlets, villages, and towns along the canal through selected development and restoration projects

- Encouragement of local business participation in the development of canal-related activities such as lodging facilities, retail stores, restaurants, and marinas
- Working cooperatively with local government in the formulation of land-use and development programs to implement the Canal Recreationway Plan
- Revitalization and protection of the commercial use of the canal, including the existing forty-seven canal terminals, which are Canal-owned docks available for commercial shipping and for use as recreational boating tie-ups
- Development of an intermodal transportation system to provide easy access to canal boating facilities, recreation centers, tourist destinations, and communities

The plan proposes using Canal Corporation funds to leverage federal, state, local, and private funds to create a $146 million investment that is expected to return in excess of $230 million in annual benefits when the plan is fully implemented. The expected benefits of further developing the canal system for recreational use include:

- 1.3 million annual visitors
- $210 million in annual revenue from canal visitors
- $8.2 million annually in state sales tax receipts
- $7.3 million annually in local sales tax receipts
- 2,700 new jobs
- $7 million annually in direct Canal Corporation revenues for reinvestment in the Canal System

The projects proposed by the plan include:

1. "Greenway" areas along the canal in four forms: corridors for wildlife / conservation, river greenways, scenic reserves, and greenways associated with and providing facilities for communities. A greenway is defined as "a protected landscape in a linear corridor of connected open spaces, incorporating natural and man-made features and including appropriate ecological, cultural, and recreational resources."

2. Improvements in accessibility to the canal, both by land and by water, including the expansion of:
   - canal access points—locations where a single activity occurs, such as a park, fishing access, or a boat launch
   - canal landings—destination points along the canal where canal-related amenities and services can be accessed. Landing projects proposed in the Canal Recreationway Plan include canal harbors, service ports and locks, and local projects. A canal harbor is a major canal port to provide boating and landside amenities at key canal locations. The seven canal harbors proposed in the plan are Little Falls, Oswego, Rochester, Seneca Falls, Tonawanda, Waterford, and Whitehall. An eighth at Syracuse is already under construction. The ninety-six service ports or locks are locations for services to boaters, hikers, cyclists, and others using the recreationway. They're spaced about every fifteen miles or less—a day of hiking or a half day's travel by boat or bike. Local projects include 515 proposals in regional canal plans for projects ranging from small canal access points to major mixed-use developments.
   - canal ports—all cities, hamlets, and villages with waterfront docking facilities along the canal such as Brockport, Spencerport, Pittsford, Fairport, Macedon, Palmyra, Newark, Lyons, Clyde, and Waterloo.
3. Pollution control activites, such as the Pure Waters programs in the Rochester-Genesee Region that help to ensure water quality and to preserve a diverse system of flora and fauna.
4. Programs to protect fish and wildlife along the canals. The plan includes provisions for clusters of development connected by stretches of undeveloped open space in areas between cities, hamlets, and villages that are conducive to the preservation of fish, waterfowl, and wildlife habitats. Other provisions consider environmental resources, including freshwater wetlands and wildlife management areas.

5. Projects to contol the future of the canals' 24,000 acres of developable land, including the use of environmental assets for purposes of natural resource protection and recreation.
6. Control of long-term use permits and short- and long-term leases, which were not permitted until the state constitution was amended.
7. Expansion and regulation of private boating activities. The 524-mile navigable canal consists of three canals in addition to the Erie Canal: the Cayuga-Seneca, Champlain, and Oswego Canals; canalized natural waterways, the central channels of Cross, Cayuga, Oneida, Onondaga, and Seneca lakes; and short canal sections at Ithaca and Watkins Glen.
8. Addition of almost 320 new miles of trailways to the existing 200-mile towpath with amenities and services to promote their use. A linear park, 524 miles long, is planned to provide a hiking-biking trail along the entire canal system. In some areas, usage includes rollerblading, horseback riding, cross-country skiing and snowmobiling.
9. Contolled fishing, hunting, and trapping.
10. Provisions to protect agricultural uses of canal land and waters, including the management of the use of canal water for farm irrigation purposes.

The canal plan recommends the development of a canal scenic byway, a network of existing roads parallel to the Canal Recreationway to be posted with consistent signs and improved for use by motorists and cyclists. It also proposes the establishment of intrepretive centers to stimulate new insights into, and heightened perception of, environmental influences on change and growth in order to enhance public understanding of how natural and man-made resources impact cultural and societal development.

The plan defines fifteen thematic regions:

- Niagara Frontier
- Ontario Lake Plan
- Metropolitan Rochester
- The Drumlins
- Cayuga-Seneca Canal
- Finger Lakes
- Gateway to the Great Lakes
- Fish and Wildlife Conservation Area
- Oneida Lake Recreation
- Upper Mohawk Valley
- Lower Mohawk Valley
- Eastern Gateway
- Upper Hudson River Valley
- Champlain Canal
- Lake Champlain

Many local projects for canal development have been proposed:

- Brockport is planning activities to draw people to the canal, including more concerts in Harvester Park, an art festival, sidewalk festivals, and the construction of boardwalks and gazebos. The *Rondout Belle* tour boat operates from Harvester Park.
- Spencerport is constructing walking trails, clearing a path and building steps to provide canal travelers access to a shopping center, building gazebos and additional facilities for boaters, and scheduling festivals and farmers' markets. The cruise ship *Celebration* operates out of Spencerport.
- Rochester will become the "Erie Harbor on the Genesee," one of the eight harbors in the canal system. The Canal Corporation's initial $5 million investment is helping the city develop a string of parks that transform Rochester into a water sports capital with recreational facilities and courses for international rowing, kayaking, and other competitions along a three-mile stretch of the Genesee River from the Erie Canal to the Court Street dam, including:

    Corn Hill Landing—infrastructure improvements and the Library Whitewater Course on the Genesee River with slalom gates, spectator areas, and a riverwalk. A launch area for hand-powered boats will be built between the canal

aqueduct and the Court Street dam. The *Sam Patch* tour boat operates from Corn Hill from Tuesday through Saturday in season.
Erie Harbor Park—a waterfront promenade along the river shoreline from Court Street to Ford Street connecting the Genesee River Trail and the Canal Trail System with downtown
Gateway Landings—A viewing area for competitive water sports
Flint Street Landing (south of Ford Street)—a mixed-use development oriented to the harbor with boat tie-up facilities and a harborfront plaza / park
Red Creek Landings (at the intersection of the Erie Canal and Red Creek)—boat docks and shoreline amentities at the location of the arched bridges across the Erie Canal
Genesee Valley Park—the site of the Watersports Center, the anchor of the southern end of the canal harbor. The park is also the northern terminus of the Greenway Project, hiking trails that link the Erie Canal to Letchworth Park and the Finger Lakes Trail to the south and the Seaway Trail to the north.

- Pittsford has completed its canalside "crown jewel" at Erie Canal Park at Schoen Place, which includes a bike trail, a dock, a pavilion, lighting, a walkway, and landscaping. A local property-owner contributed $40,000 to augment a $75,000 state grant to develop a waterfront park. The *Sam Patch* tour boat operates from Schoen Place on Sundays in season.
- Fairport is a model for canalside development. Since 1981 the Fairport Industrial Development Agency has invested more than $1 million in canal-related improvements, converting a former industrial park to a scenic, welcoming place for canal travelers. The village established jogging and biking trails and created linear parks along the canal that include electrical service and benches,

signs, lighting, and other amenities. Also, Fairport converted an old box factory on the canal into a building housing a boat rental office, corporate offices, small businesses, and a restaurant. The tour boats *Colonial Belle* and *Fairport Lady* operate from Fairport in season. Mid-Lakes Navigation's *Evita II* operates from Fairport in May and early June.

- Macedon is focusing on natural beauty and trails. The town is developing a greenway linear park along Route 31 and trails along the towpath as part of a countywide system of trails along former railroad beds. Volunteers have built trails connecting eastern Monroe and western Wayne counties. Bullis Park and Canal Park are being improved, including the addition of gazebos and a handicapped-accessible fishing dock.
- Palmyra is using a $10,000 grant from the Canal Corporation to attract private development and matching municipal funds to develop a canal-front marina and a visitor center. The master plan includes the identification of walking tours of downtown historic areas and revitalization of the business district.
- Newark plans to develop a village center focused on the canal. An initial grant of $58,000 is being used to provide enhancements such as benches, signs, and fuel stations and pump-out stations for boats.
- Lyons is developing the Erie Canal Cultural Center in the former Hamett paper factory. The cultural canter is a cooperative effort of the county, town, and village coordinated by the Wayne County Council on the Arts. It includes the Lyons library, space for art exhibitions by the historical society, a performing arts center, work spaces for artists, and a center for art classes.
- Clyde is planning "the gateway to the natural areas of the East" from the village through the great swamplands of the Montezuma National Wildlife Refuge. Clyde's Erie Canal Park Committee plans walking and biking trails, parks for picnics, hunting and fishing areas, serene waters for canoeing, boating tie-ups, and a natural amphitheatre

with an area for a barge to tie-up and present concerts near an expanded festival grounds.

- Geneva is developing its lakefront on Seneca Lake, including a large new hotel and biking and hiking trails. The Finger Lakes Interpretive Center, which is expected to attract 50,000 visitors annually, will be built near the entrance to Seneca Lake State Park. It will include an auditorium, computerized interpretive displays, video presentations, and exhibits about science, technology, and agriculture.
- Waterloo, on the Cayuga-Seneca Canal, used a state grant of $88,200, village labor, and volunteer labor to transform Oak Island into a welcoming area for the village. Oak Island provides docking areas for boaters including a handicapped-accessible dock, picnic areas, and a trail that includes a walking tour of the village.
- Seneca Falls, also on the Cayuga-Seneca Canal, used a $67,800 grant from the Canal Corporation to install information kiosks and wayside exhibits throughout its Urban Cultural Park and to construct a lighted overlook of the "lost village" beneath the canal in Van Cleef Lake. Seneca Falls will become a harbor in the Canal Recreational Plan and will use $4 million in Canal Corporation funds and $2.6 million in other grants to become a "Gateway to the Finger Lakes." The harbor will have a boats-for-hire terminal and amenities for visitors and will link the canal to the Women's Rights National Historic Park, the National Women's Hall of Fame, and other historic sites in the village. The harbor is expected to attract 200,000 annually to Seneca Falls.
- Syracuse is developing Syracuse Inner Harbor that adjoins Onondaga Lake and the Erie and Oswego Canals. The federal government, the Thruway Authority, and the city of Syracuse are using $19.5 million to build an aquarium, marina, restaurant, and shopping complex. Syracuse already has the Erie Canal Museum, a gem of a museum.

New York State has an outstanding plan for the recreational and economic use of its canals. Finally, an incredible resource in our backyards is going to be used to its potential. However, of the two tasks, planning and implementing, implementing is frequently the more difficult.

In August 1996, Howard Steinberg, who succeeded Peter Tufo as Thruway Authority Chairman the preceding January, scaled down Tufo's fifteen-year, $146 million Canal Recreationway Plan to a five-year, $32.3 million plan. The revised plan focuses on four elements: canal harbors, service port and lock projects, the canalway trail, and a canal-system marketing plan. The revised plan also provides for basic boating services and improving access to the 524-mile canal system. The revised plan provides for building a 70-mile trail along the Erie Canal and the improvement of forty locks. The development of eight canal harbors across the state is unaffected by the new plan.

In the opinion of Keith Giles, Canal Corporation director and chief engineer, the five-year project should be viewed as the first phase of a long-term effort to achieve the goals of the Recreationway Plan. He said, "We will re-evaluate the program in five years, if it is successful, we will continue on and eventually complete the whole master plan." The canal plan will be funded by boater tolls, other canal fees, and $10 million in federal aid. No money from Thruway tolls will be used for canal improvements, as proposed in the original plan.

Much hard work remains to be accomplished; however, it must be done. In commenting on the popularity of the canal, William C. Warren III, a member of the Canal Recreationway Committee, observed that "the canal is accessible, it's safe, it offers a wide range of opportunities, it has great historical meaning, and it's very beautiful." Warren's observations provide the justification for further recreational and economic development of the canal.

◆ ◆ ◆

Lock 26, Clyde

Main Street, Fairport

Bibliography

Adams, Samuel Hopkins. *Grandfather Stories*. New York: Random House, 1955.

Andrist, Ralph K. *The Erie Canal*. New York: American Heritage, 1964.

Blackwell, Jeffrey. "Adams Basin." Rochester *Democrat and Chronicle*. 14 Aug. 1995: 3B.

Bobbé, Dorothie. *DeWitt Clinton*. New York: Putnam, 1968.

Bourne, Russell. *Floating West: The Erie and Other American Canals*. New York: Norton, 1992.

Chalmers, Harvey II. *The Birth of the Erie Canal*. New York: Bookman, 1960.

Cho, Janet H. and Jack Jones. "The Canal's Past: A Voyage Back Through Time." Rochester *Democrat and Chronicle*. 7 June 1994: 1A, 4-5A.

Doherty, John. "State Scales Back Canal Tourism Plan." Syracuse *Post-Standard*. 22 Aug. 1996: B-7.

Drago, Harry Sinclair. *Canal Days in America: The History and Romance of Old Towpaths and Waterways*. New York: Bramhall House, 1972.

Edmonds, Walter D. *Erie Water*. Boston: Little, Brown, 1933.

---. *Mostly Canallers: Collected Stories*. Boston: Little, Brown, 1934.

Eldredge, Mary Louise, ed. *Pioneers of Macedon*. Macedon Center, NY: n.p., 1975.

Finch, Roy. G. *The Story of the New York State Canals: Historical and Commercial Information*. Albany: n.p., 1925.

Fitzgerald, John R. *The New Erie Canal: A Recreational Guide*. N.p., n.p., 1993.

Franchere, Ruth. *Westward by Canal*. New York: Macmillan, 1972.

Frankel, Jeremy G. and Peter Wiles. Jr., *New York State Canal Guide: Everything the Canaller Needs to Know and More*. Skaneateles, NY: Mid-Lakes Navigation, n.d.

Garrity, Richard. *Canal Boatman: My Life on Upstate Waterways*. Syracuse: Syracuse UP, 1977.

Geddes, George. *Origin and History of the Measures That Led to the Construction of the Erie Canal*. Syracuse: Summers, 1866.

Hall, Edith, ed. *The History of Baldwinsville*. Baldwinsville, NY: n.p., 1936.

Hart, Isabella H. *History of Pittsford, New York*. Pittsford, NY: n.p., 1970.

Jones, Jack. "The Canal's Future: A look into the Possibilities of the Canal." Rochester *Democrat and Chronicle*. 8 June 1994: 1A, 6-7A.

Klees, Emerson. *Persons, Places, and Things Around the Finger Lakes Region;* Rochester, NY: Friends of the Finger Lakes Publishing, 1994.

---. *Persons, Places, and Things In the Finger Lakes Region*. Rochester, NY: Friends of the Finger Lakes Publishing, 1993.

Merrill, Arch. *The Towpath*. Rochester, NY: *Democrat and Chronicle*, 1945.

Mintz, Max M. *Gouverneur Morris and the American Revolution*. Norman: U of Oklahoma P, 1970.

New York State Canal Recreationway Commission. "New York State Recreationway Plan." Albany: n.p., 1995.

Orr, Jim. "Life on the Canal: Dreams Abound on the Erie." Rochester *Democrat and Chronicle*. 6 June 1994: 1A, 3-5A.

Rapp, Marvin A. *Canal Water and Whiskey: Tall Tales from the Erie Canal Country*. New York, Twayne, 1965.

Sesquicentennial Committee, Town of Ogden and Village of Spencerport. *150 Years in Ogden, 100 Years in Spencerport*. Spencerport, NY: n.p., 1967.

Shaw, Ronald E. *Canals for a Nation: The Canal Era in the United States 1790-1860*. Lexington: U of Kentucky P, 1990.

State Engineer and Surveyor of the State of New York. *Supplement to the Annual Report*. Albany: Brandow, 1906.

Stelter, John H. "Jesse Hawley, Erie Canal Publicist and Freemason." *Transactions of the American Lodge of Research—Free and Accepted Masons*. Vol. XIV, No. 3, 1980.

Thompson, Harold W. *Body, Boots & Britches: Folktales, Ballads, and Speech from Country New York*. New York: Dover, 1967.

Wolf, Doris. "One Man's Vision: There's Money to Be Made on the Canal." Rochester *Democrat and Chronicle*. 7 July 1995: 1A, 6A.

---. "Locking in the Future: Master Plan for Erie Canal Uses History to Direct Path of Growth." Rochester *Democrat and Chronicle*. 12 July 1995: 1E, 4E.

Wolfe, Andrew D. "Can Erie Canal Plan Create a Newer, Better New York?" Brighton-Pittsford *Post*. 19 July 1995: 1-2.

---. "Erie Canal: Millions of Visitors a Year?" Brighton-Pittsford *Post*. 15 May 1996: 1, 4.

Wyld, Lionel D. *Boaters and Broomsticks: Tales & Historical Lore of the Erie Canal*. Utica: North Country Books, 1986.

---. *Low Bridge! Folklore and the Erie Canal*. Syracuse: Syracuse UP, 1962.

Waterway Crane, Lock 25, Mays Point

Index

Adams Basin, 64-65
Alasa Farms, 124
Albany, 8, 10, 12, 20, 34, 37, 64, 83, 88
Alling Coverlet Museum, 73, 105-106
Amberg Wine Cellars, 126
Antique / Classic Boat Show, 178
Aqueduct Park, 73
Auburn, 45, 85, 160-161, 166
Auburn Concert Series, 177
Austin Park, 182, 187
Baldwin, Dr. Jonas C., 79
Baldwinsville, 79
Baltimore Woods, 182, 187
Barrow, John D., 182, 188-189
Bates, David Stanhope, 30
Bayard, Stephen, 3
Beaver Lake Nature Center, 183
Belhurst Castle, 135-136
Blue Cut Nature Center, 76, 119-120
Brewerton, 80-81
Broadhead, Charles C., 29
Brockport, 60-63, 64, 193, 202, 204
Brockway, Hiel, 60, 61
Bushnells Basin, 69
Buffalo, 3, 8, 10, 20, 37, 64, 83, 88, 92, 193
Camillus Erie Canal Park, v, 185
Canalboat, 10, 31
Canal Commission, 4, 24, 29, 60
Canandaigua, 16, 19, 21, 85, 92-94, 99, 109
Canandaigua *Genesee Messenger*, 21
Canandaigua Lady, 110
Canandaigua Lake State Marine Park, 104
Canandaigua Speedway, 110
Captain Gray's Boat Tours, 111
Carpenter's Brook Fish Hatchery, 186
Casey Park, 160, 176
Cayuga Community College, 176
Cayuga Community College Trail, 177
Cayuga County, iii, 60, 78, 86
Cayuga County Agricultural Museum, 160, 171
Cayuga County Fair Speedway, 165
Cayuga Lake, 10, 12, 78, 79, 86, 203
Cayuga Lake State Park, 151
Cayuga Museum of History and Art, 160, 171
Cayuga-Seneca Canal, 12, 78, 143, 203, 204, 207
Celebration, 204
Centreport Aqueduct, xiv
Champlain Canal, 12, 19, 203, 204
Chancey, Commodore Isaac, 87
Chimney Bluffs State Park, 86, 122
Chittenango, 9, 28
Clinton, DeWitt, 4, 7, 10, 16-18, 22, 24, 27
Clinton, George, 2, 16
Clyde, 25, 44, 77-78, 86, 123, 202, 206
Clyde River, 12, 26, 78, 123
Cohoes Falls, 3
Colden, Cadwallader, 2, 21
Colles, Christopher, 2, 21
Colonial Belle, 206
Convention Days, 157
DeLand, Daniel, 70
Denonville, Marquis, 86, 87, 99
DeZeng, Frederick, 77
DeWitt, Simeon, 3, 4, 16, 18, 19, 20
Dickens, Charles, 35
DIRT Motorsport Hall of Fame and Classic Car Collection, 165
Durham Boats, 20
Eddy, Thomas, 3, 4
Electronics Communications Museum, 98
Elizabeth Cady Stanton House, 146
Emerson Park, 160, 177
Empire State Farm Days, 157
Erie Canal Act, 22
Erie Canal Guide, iii
Erie Canal Museum, 31, 185, 207

Evita II, 206
Fair Haven Beach State Park, 161-162
Fairport, 70-71, 202, 205
Fairport Lady, 206
Finger Lakes Antique Car Show, 178
Finger Lakes Community College, 92, 104, 109
Finger Lakes Performing Arts Center, 92, 109
Finger Lakes Race Track, 92, 112
Forman, Joshua, 4, 16, 21
Fort Hill Cemetery, 160, 166
Fort Stanwix (Rome), 2
Galen Marsh State Wildife Management Center, 123
Ganargua Creek, 73, 74, 76
Ganondagan State Historic Site, 87, 99
Geddes, James, 3, 4, 9, 17, 18-19, 26, 29, 30
Genesee River, 10, 30, 67, 204, 205
Geneva, 19, 20, 85, 118-119, 127, 134, 207
Geneva-on-the-Lake Resort, 137-139
Ginna (Robert E.) Nuclear Power Plant, 95
Granger Homestead and Carriage Museum, 92, 99-100
Hardenburgh, John L., 160
Harris, Martin, 108
Hawley, Jesse, 3, 16, 17, 19-23
Hill Cumorah, 106, 109, 112-113
Historic Grandin Building, 108
Hobart / William Smith Colleges, 118, 128
Hoffman Clock Museum, 75, 126
Holloway House, 115
Holley, Myron, 60, 73
Hotchkiss, H. G., 76
Howland Island State Wildlife Management Area, 162-163
Hudson River, 3, 7, 10, 16, 19, 20, 21, 23, 24, 25, 29, 204
Hydraulic Cement, 9, 28
Irish Canal Workers, 8, 27, 44, 56-57
Irondequoit River, 10, 30, 86
Iroquois Confederation, 16, 92, 166
Iroquois Museum (Owasco Teyetasta), 171
Jefferson, Thomas, 1, 4, 24
Jervis, John B. , 29
Jordan, 60, 78, 86
Kershaw Park, 104
The Krebs, 182, 195-196
Lake Erie, 3, 4, 10, 16, 18, 19, 20, 21, 23, 24, 25, 26, 85, 87
Lake Ontario, 4, 19, 21, 49, 84, 85, 86, 87
Lake Shore Marshes Wildlife Management Area, 145
Languedoc Canal, 9
Liberty Erie Canal Cruises, 125
Little Falls, 3, 79, 202
Lock 23, Brewerton, 81
Lock 24, Baldwinsville, 80
Lock 25, Mays Point, 78
Lock 26, Clyde, 77, 78
Lock 27, Lyons, 76, 77
Lock 28A, Lyons, 77
Lock 28B, Newark, 75
Lock 29, Palmyra, 73
Lock 30, Macedon, 72
Lock 32, Pittsford, 67
Lock 33, Henrietta, 67
Lockport, 10, 22, 23, 26, 34
Logan, Chief (Tah-gah-jute), 166
Lyons, 50, 76-77, 86, 202, 206
McCormick, Cyrus, 61, 62
Macedon, 71-72, 73, 86, 202, 206
Madison, James, 4, 17, 25, 87
Memorial Day Museum, 144, 155-156
Merry-Go-Round-Playhouse, 177-178
Mid-Lakes Navigation, Ltd., 192-193
Mike Weaver Drain Tile Museum, 132
Mohawk River, 3, 8, 12, 16, 20, 29, 79, 204
Monroe County, iii, 60
Montezuma Marshes, 10, 25, 44, 49
Montezuma National Wildlife Refuge, 44, 78, 151-153, 193, 206
Moore, Sir Henry, 2, 21
Moroni Monument, 106-107
Morris, Gouverneur, 4, 16, 21, 23-25

Morrison, Samuel Eliot, 5
Mynderse, Colonel Wilhelminus, 20, 143
National Women's Hall of Fame, 142, 147, 207
New York Chiropractic College, 151
The New Erie Canal, iii
New York Pageant of Steam, 110
New York State Barge Canal System, 12, 13
New York State Canal Recreationway Commission, 200, 208
New York State Canal Recreational Plan, 200, 202, 208
New York State Thruway, 12, 85, 86, 200, 207, 208
Newark, 74-75, 86, 127, 193, 202, 206
Nine Mile Creek Aqueduct, 6
North, William, 4
Old Erie Canal State Park, 60
Oliver Loud's Inn, 69
Oneida Lake, 19, 20, 60, 78, 79, 80, 81, 203, 204
Oneida River, 12, 79, 80
Onondaga County, iii, 60, 78, 85, 86
Onondaga Lake, 80
Ontario County Historical Society Museum, 92, 102
Oswego River, 12, 19, 80, 81
Owasco Teyetasta (Iroquois Museum), 171
Palmyra, 72-74, 86, 193, 202, 206
Palmyra Historical Museum, 106
Peppermint, 76
Persons, Places, and Things Around the Finger Lakes Region, iii, 84
Persons, Places, and Things In the Finger Lakes Region, iii
Pittsford, 68, 202, 205
Platt, Jonas, 3
Port Byron, 60, 78, 86
Port Gibson, 74
Porter, Peter B., 4
Power, Tyrone, 55
Prouty-Chew Museum, 118, 128-129
Pultneyville, 88
Richardson's Canal House, 69
Roberts, Nathan, 10, 25-27, 30
Rochester, 10, 22, 25, 30, 61, 67, 84, 86, 92, 93, 202, 204
Rolling Wheels Track, 190
Rome, 4, 8, 9, 20, 25, 28, 29, 60, 81
Rondout Belle, 204
Rose Hill Mansion, 118, 129-132
The Sacred Cove, 109
St. Lawrence Seaway, 12
Sam Patch, 205
Sauerkraut Festival, 133
Schenectady, 34
Schoen Place, v, 68, 205
Schweinfurth Memorial Art Center, 160, 172
Schuyler, Philip, 2, 21, 24
Scythe Tree, 144, 154-155
Seneca Chief, 10, 11, 18, 22
Seneca Dreamer, 135
Seneca Falls, 20, 142-143, 146, 202, 207
Seneca Falls Historical Society Museum, 150-151
Seneca Lake, 12, 29, 78, 203, 207
Seneca Lake State Park, 118, 127, 207
Seneca River, 8, 12, 20, 25, 44, 80, 81
Seward House, 160, 167-170
Seymour, James, 60
Sherwood Inn, 182, 197, 198
Skaneateles, 85, 182-183, 187
Skaneateles Art Exhibition, 190
The Skaneateles Festival, 182, 190
Skaneateles Historical Association Museum, 189-190
Skaneateles Nature Trail, 182, 188
Skaneateles Polo Club, 182, 191
Smith, Joseph, 108, 109
Smith Opera House, 118, 134-135
Sodus Bay Lighthouse Museum, 120
Sodus Point, 88
Sodus Shaker Festival, 124-125
Sonnenberg Gardens and Mansion, 92, 102-104
Spencer, Daniel, 66
Spencerport, 64, 65-66, 202, 204

Springside Inn, 178-179
Stanton, Elizabeth Cady, 142, 146, 147
Sterling Renaissance Festival, 164
Stump Puller, 8, 53, 54
Syracuse, 9, 12, 18, 25, 28, 29, 60, 84, 85, 86, 92, 185, 193, 207
Thayer Park, 182, 188
Thendara Inn, 111
Thomas, David, 26, 30
Thorpe Vineyard and Farm Winery, 145
Three Rivers State Wildlife Management Area, 184
Thruway 2000, 200
Tompkins, Daniel, 4, 17
Tour Boats, 110, 111, 125, 135, 192, 204, 205, 206
Tubman, Harriet, 170
Urban Cultural Park—Village of Seneca Falls, 149-150
Utica, 4, 9, 16, 20, 81
Valentown Museum of Local History, 96-98
Van Cortlandt, General, 3
Van Renssalaer, Jeremiah, 3
Van Renssalaer, Stephen, 4
Victor, 87
War of 1812, 87
Washington, George, 21, 64, 92
Waterloo, 85, 143-144, 202, 207
Watson, Elkanah, 2, 3, 21
Wayne County, iii, 46, 60, 86, 206
Wayne County Historial Society Museum, 122
Weedsport, 60, 78, 86
Western Inland Lock Navigation Company, 3, 20, 29, 79
Wesleyan Chapel, 142, 149
Weston, William, 4, 29
White, Canvass, 9, 27-28, 30
Wild Water Derby, 114-115
Willard Memorial Chapel, 160, 161, 173-176
William Phelps General Store Museum, 106
Williamson International Speedway, 96
Whitmer, Peter, 155
Wood Creek, 2, 3, 16, 20, 29, 79
Wooden Toy Factory, 186-187
Women's Rights National Historical Park Visitor Center, 142, 147, 207
Wright, Benjamin, 3, 9, 25, 27, 29-30
Yeo, Commodore Sir James, 87, 88